A B L B H

A Better Life: Brianna's Hope

Recovery Conversations

with Randy Davis

Volume 1

Published by Happy Owl Publishing, LLC

ISBN - 979-8-8508661-3-6

Edited and formatted by J.D. Upchurch

Cover Art by Natalie Haymore

Transcriptions by Kandi Sapp

Website Design by Regina Raines

For more information, and to purchase additional copies, visit our website www.RecoveryConversations.org

Contact Randy Davis or ABLBH by email: www.info@ablbh.org

CONTENTS

Impact of ABLBH

"The guest speakers A Better Life - Brianna's Hope brought to our high school made powerful and insightful connections with our students through their personal stories of addiction and recovery. The need for ABLBH's outreach in our schools was brought home to me as I observed a convocation with Randy and his guests at our high school. Randy asked the several hundred students assembled in our school auditorium to raise their hands if they had a family member or know someone who is struggling with addiction. I watched as the hands of so many of our kids shot up across the auditorium. Clearly, many of our students are living with the impacts of addiction in their lives, or in the lives of those they care most about."

Jeremy Gulley, Superintendent, Jay School Corporation

"The unique approach of A Better Life - Brianna's Hope to help those struggling with addiction is a breath of fresh air. It was at a meeting in New Castle, Indiana that I recognized this organization's selfless efforts on behalf of those battling substance abuse."

Bishop Julius Trimble, United Methodist Church, IN

"I have been adopted into the Brianna's Hope family and it has changed my life. I'm no longer just clean and sober; I'm now in recovery."

A grateful recovering addict

"Listening to the *Faith In Your Recovery* podcast is like opening an envelope, taking out the contents, and sorting through a personal life. It amazes me how God can turn a life around."

A podcast listener

"Brianna's Hope funded me for my five-day detox and then for a twenty-eight-day residential treatment which began my sobriety. More importantly, they believed in me, not once, but twice, when I didn't believe in myself. They left me with no excuse but to go to treatment. Their initial funding allowed me to sit still long enough to believe I could do recovery."

Dustin, an ABLBH client

Preface

This collection of stories is one way A Better Life - Brianna's Hope is attacking the stigma and bias associated with substance use disorder. The American Medical Association identifies addiction as a disease, though many still believe it is a choice. In this book, we are not attempting to win the argument of whether addiction is a disease or a choice. We simply want to share personal experiences that speak to the pain, loss, struggles, emptiness, and separation that accompany addiction. Through transcribed interviews from the *Faith In Your Recovery* podcast, we will introduce you to some amazing people that have life-changing stories about addiction and recovery. The interviews are presented as they were originally conducted, with minor grammatical changes for clarity. These changes do not alter the meaning of the interviews but rather make them more easily readable.

We believe that *Recovery Conversations with Randy Davis* will challenge your present point of view and help you look more open-mindedly at people with addiction. You will read how some began their addiction as the result of reliance on opioid pain medication that was originally prescribed to help them. Others met their addictions at parties and as a way of finding social connections. Peer pressure drew many into the darkness. Some were introduced to alcohol or drugs by their own parents. These stories include the interviews of those that personally struggled with an addiction resulting in job losses, overdose scares, jail time, and isolation, but are now on the road to recovery. Other stories you will read are from those that have lost loved ones to addiction and are still trying to make sense of it all. Our goal is that you gain a deeper understanding of the struggle and a renewed appreciation for the struggler. At A Better Life - Brianna's Hope and in the *Faith In Your Recovery* podcast, we don't claim to have all the answers to this issue. Sometimes we aren't even sure what questions to ask. However, we do believe we have allowed, encouraged, and empowered many to find their own answers. Since our beginning on November 5, 2014, we have witnessed untold numbers of lives touched, changed, and even saved.

Λ Better Life - Brianna's Hope is a non-profit, faith-based—not faith-forced—organization. We will not say you must have God to make it out of addiction, but our experience has proven that you stand a far better chance with Him. Stay in the battle!

Chapter One

Brianna's Story and Ours

Randy Davis is a retired pastor, founder of A Better Life - Brianna's Hope, and the host of the *Faith In Your Recovery* podcast. In this chapter, you will read more about Randy and the inspirations and motivations behind his work. He will also share the story of Brianna, the woman whose life and final letter led to the creation of A Better Life - Brianna's Hope.

RANDY: Hey there. Thanks for joining us. Are you tired of the fight? Fed up with the struggle? Done lying to yourself about the next time? Hold on. We don't believe you've come this far to only come this far. Whether you stumbled onto our podcast and this story or connected intentionally, we think you may be where the next step of your recovery is about to happen. *Faith In Your Recovery* may be just what you need. We have become a true source of help and hope for those battling SUD—substance use disorder. We also call that addiction. Those strugglers were once forgotten, cast out, and discarded. They're now proving to each other, and to everyone else, that recovery is possible. Where negativity, desperation, and hopelessness once lived, there is now a path to a healthy and successful future. After airing more than sixty episodes, this one has a bit of a twist. After over fourteen months of providing programs, we've grown in listener numbers and outreach. Today, we want to remind you who we are and what we are about. We're going to turn the tables—or maybe I should say the microphones—and instead of me doing the interview, I'm going to be interviewed by Rob Spalding. He's a friend and the executive director of the Christian Center here in Anderson, Indiana. It is in their studio, with the help of Eric Foley, that we produce our podcast. We want to introduce, or reintroduce you to our parent organization, A Better Life - Brianna's Hope, and then we'll talk about the wonderful things God is doing with our podcast, *Faith In Your Recovery*. Rob, thanks for helping us out.

ROB: Thank you for having me. Or in this case, I guess I'm having you since I am assuming the role of host.

RANDY: Hey, you're the boss today, all right? What a responsibility. Introduce yourself to the folks. Tell them a little more about yourself.

ROB: Yes, thank you, Randy. First, it is a real honor to be here. I love the podcast and the work you do, so this is an honor to interview you. Thank you for the invitation.

RANDY: Well, I appreciate your willingness to help accomplish this. I think it's important that we inform the folks of who we are, what we're about, and what we can offer. We want to introduce them to Brianna's story, as well as to our past, our present, and our plans for the future.

ROB: That's awesome. First, who am I? My name is Rob Spalding, and I'm the executive director of the Christian Center Rescue Ministry. We have about a dozen different services that we provide to people all over east-central Indiana, and we are truly thankful for the opportunity to do that. I was born and raised in central Indiana. My background is in finance, accounting, and all those things that you would never expect of somebody who is running a homeless shelter and a sober living facility. But that's my background. I've lived here forever, and like most people we know, addictions have touched my life and the lives of those in my family. I view this as a great opportunity to have this conversation and talk about what you guys are doing and the great work that is going on.

RANDY: Sounds like it is going to be an interesting time here. I'm looking forward to it. Here we go. Have at it. You open a door and I'll walk through it.

ROB: Great. Let's start with your background. Randy, I'd like to hear your story and some of the things that have gotten you to this point in your life. I am curious to discover what has motivated you, not just to start A Better Life - Brianna's Hope, but also the podcast and all the other things that are going on.

RANDY: My motivation comes mainly from God and the way He has given me a passion to reach out to the underdog and the struggler. I've always been blessed—not necessarily with wealth, though I've never been without a meal or roof—but I've been blessed to experience life as I have, and I want to see other folks lifted up and encouraged. I want to see them helped and for them to become the persons God created them to be.

ROB: Right, because those underdogs all have a story, don't they?

RANDY: Oh, I love those stories. They're inspirational to me. This isn't me reaching down to them. We're just reaching across the table to one another when we do this.

ROB: Amen. And one thing that's important about that is once you've learned someone's story, it's hard to judge them, isn't it?

RANDY: You cannot tell your story without telling the story of others. There's always a head nodding in agreement, as if to say, "Yeah, I've been there. I've done that. And these friends of mine get it." Even those of us who have not been where they have been need to know what that life is about if we are going to respect them as we should.

I am from Delaware County and a graduate of Delta High School. I spent two years at Ball State University, and a couple of years in the US Army, stationed in Frankfort, Germany as a finance clerk. I received my Advanced Individual Training at Fort Benjamin Harrison in Indianapolis.

ROB: That's impressive.

RANDY: It was a great experience and something my maturity needed at that time in my life. I am thankful for it. I was attending Ball State University. My brother had just been drafted and was going to Vietnam. That's one of the reasons I went to Ball State. I wanted the deferment that college allowed. But, with him going to Nam, I knew they wouldn't send me as well. Without any true college plans or direction, I stepped away from Ball State University, where I was majoring in radio and television broadcasting, and joined the Army. That became fourteen months of what I needed. I was able to travel and enjoy so much. I came home for my wedding, and then my wife was able to go back to Germany with me. It was a great experience. Following my discharge, I fumbled around through several different jobs, including construction. My dad was a contractor. At the age of thirty-three, I found a calling and a home in pulpit ministry, pastoring a church. That calling gave me a chance to exercise and learn a greater and deeper love for people and their experiences. I loved my ministry opportunities and the relationships they provided. I did that for the next thirty-five years. Then, in July 2018, I retired. However, prior to that, I was involved in a project we called Veterans' Gift Cards. We would collect funds of about five dollars apiece, then go out and buy McDonald's gift cards. Then we would present them to veterans at VA hospitals throughout Indiana, at parades, legions, and wherever we could find a veteran. Besides just giving them the cards, we'd listen to their stories. That inspired me to realize I had more in me. So, I stepped away from that, and within three months, a young lady in our area by the name of Brianna DeBattiste was reported as missing. That was the moment of conception leading to the creation of A Better Life - Brianna's Hope.

ROB: I would love for you to share more about Brianna and that connection. Listening to your podcast I always had the sense that it's very personal.

RANDY: I hope so. I am from Redkey, a rural community in east central Indiana. It is a community of thirteen hundred if everybody's home. I live within a mile of the town. My wife, Rose, was a first-grade teacher in Albany, Indiana. One night, via Facebook, we received word that Brianna had disappeared. No one knew any details at that point or had any clues about what was going on. Brianna's aunt, who lived just a couple of fields from us, had been in my wife's class in her second year of teaching. I immediately contacted her. We also knew some of her other family members. I asked them if I, as a pastor, could come alongside them to encourage, help, and walk with them; to be there. They were more than happy to take advantage of the offer. That forever changed my life. As I said, that was about four years before my retirement. Right up to that moment, I had thought retirement was going to be putting my rear end in a La-Z-Boy. God had other plans and mine were not going to happen. Prior to Brianna's disappearance on June 16, 2014, I had connected with her twice by visiting her in the Jay County Jail. Her mother had called and said, "She's in again for drug charges. Would you go speak to her?" I went to speak to her both times, but that is where our relationship and connection ended. It was ten weeks after Brianna's disappearance that her body was located. It was laying atop the ground, covered over with brush. The brush proved she didn't get there by herself. The location was an abandoned cemetery in the western part of Jay County near Ridgeville, Indiana. To be frank, when her body was found, one arm, one hand, and her head were missing. Now, let me explain that. There were enough gnaw marks present that we know it was the varmints and critters that did the physical damage. After all, her body had been in this wooded area for all that time. I want to be clear that it was not decapitation by anyone. To this day, no one has stepped up to say they were involved or to describe her final moments. Law enforcement diligently sought answers, but they never could find that piece of evidence, that smoking gun, to confidently charge somebody in any way with this. It is believed that her demise was due to her drug issues. Brianna's battle with drugs began in seventh grade. By her senior year—though she was a homecoming queen candidate, known as a friend to the friendless, and an aspiring fashion designer—there wasn't a drug she wasn't using. By the time she was twenty-five—which was her age at death—she was a full-blown heroin addict. To the best of anyone's knowledge, it is believed that she went to a party and overdosed. Whether it was forced on her or voluntary, we do not know at this point. It is believed that someone panicked, took her body, and hid it where it was found on September 1, 2014.

ROB: So, someone's daughter, just thrown away?

RANDY: There's no better way to put it, as harsh as that sounds folks. That is exactly what happened. It was discarded and abandoned like trash. It wasn't of enough value to even dump in someone's yard where she would at least be found.

ROB: That is just incomprehensibly tragic.

RANDY: It was—and I don't want to say there was an upside to the loss—but one good thing that came out of it was simply that after her story was told three times, on the front page of The Muncie Star, Jay County, Indiana could no longer proclaim, "We don't have a problem."

ROB: Isn't it a typical thought that the small towns—like Scottsburg and Redkey and others in Indiana, and all across the country—don't have drug problems? We want to believe this is just a big city problem.

RANDY: Oh, absolutely. Over the eight years I have been involved with this, we have been in two communities that made that clear. In the words of one community, "We don't need your kind." They meant recovery programs. Basically, they were saying, "We do not need your kind in our community because of the reputation it will give us." It made no sense then, and it still doesn't. The other community made it quite clear they didn't have a problem. My biggest mistake, Rob, was not inviting them to travel around with me and tell others how their community could get through this epidemic without having an addiction problem. That was as much denial as anybody's ever had in addiction.

ROB: Right, and that plays a major role in the problem. I am talking about the denial and ignoring of this because, "It happened to this young lady, but it couldn't possibly happen in my community." So, after ten weeks Brianna's body was found and then there was a memorial service?

RANDY: Yes. The service was held in the first part of October 2014. She disappeared on June 16th of 2014. Her body was found on September 1st, and the memorial service was held on October 3rd. In three hours, 450-500 individuals came through for the viewing. Due to the condition of her body, it was a closed casket kind of thing. My opinion is that of 450-500 individuals, one-third of them got home not knowing where they had been. You know, you could tell by the glassed-over look in the eyes as well as other hints. The evidence of their condition and lack of sobriety

16

was easily noticed. But I get it. How does someone who struggles with addiction muster up the strength to go see a friend in a casket or see their picture for the final time without that drug they've depended on for so long?

ROB: Something drew them there.

RANDY: Yes, the closeness of the addiction community and the reminder that this could be any one of them, possibly next. It was personal to so many.

ROB: Trauma plays such a big role in addiction, and I think one of the things we must remember is that often the addict has a significant amount of trauma in their past and possibly present. These are broken people that behave like broken people.

RANDY: Absolutely, and drugs are their escape until they learn a better, healthier way to get away from it.

ROB: Yes. So, tell me, how did the first meeting of A Better Life - Brianna's Hope unfold?

RANDY: That happened November 5, 2014, in Redkey, Indiana.

ROB: So, you didn't waste any time.

RANDY: We tried to make it happen as quickly as reasonably possible.

ROB: So, a month after her memorial service you're having your first meeting?

RANDY: Yes, a month and two days.

ROB: That's incredible.

RANDY: It was a fresh thing, and everybody was hurting. The community was clamoring and asking, "What are we going to do to keep this from happening again?" After working it out with the family, we were able to hold our first meeting of A Better Life - Brianna's Hope at what was then a former bank building that had been vacated. We had twenty-two individuals show up that night. That was more than we expected. It eventually grew to over eighty in that small building. That is when individuals started stepping up and asking, "Hey, can I take this to my hometown? I'll lead a group." We offered training to help them have the best possible start and make the greatest difference they could make, and that's how we rolled. I have always believed a sloppy start is better than no start.

ROB: What are the framework, the guidelines, and the standards for a meeting?

RANDY: I'll even describe a meeting to you here in a moment, though like any group, no two meetings are the same. However, we did throw in unifying and similar experiences and methods for each chapter. In our identity statement, we call ourselves, "A participant-driven, faith-based, compassion-filled, support and recovery movement for those battling the battle with substance use disorder/addiction." It is important to mention our foundational document, which we call "Brianna's Prayer." Brianna's Prayer was written by Brianna. Three days before her body was located, her mother found it in some of her personal belongings. She shared it with me, and we have adopted it as a major part of every meeting we have. I'd like to share it with you folks. Remember, this is from one of those individuals that was called a worthless junkie, whose body was discarded and thrown away like trash. These are her words:

> "Please Lord, look after me and my family. Please
> help me to do the right thing and to show people
> I'm not a bad person inside or out and help me Lord
> to get through this disappointment again and know
> I make mistakes but who doesn't? I don't do it to
> do wrong. I do it cuz I feel I have no other
> choice. I want a better life, Lord, I do. Please help
> me. Do to me as what you feel is best. I surrender
> to you. In Jesus' name, Amen."
> (Shared exactly as written by Brianna.)

ROB: That's powerful because that sounds like a lot of people have that same prayer.

RANDY: It fits a lot of lives. As an element of our meetings, this prayer is a must. This prayer must be shared. It can be done at the start, middle, or end of the meeting. It can be on the screen. It can be on handouts. It can be one person reading it or saying it from memory. It can be in unison. We don't care. We do not want a chapter meeting, gathering, or even a board meeting without this prayer being shared. As I said earlier, it is the foundational document that binds our organization together as one. Our mission statement—though not used as much as our identity statement—reads, "Providing hope through Christ to individuals and communities battling addiction using support, encouragement, and collaboration." We continue to remind folks we are faith-based, not faith-forced or faith-expected. We're going to live our faith. You can live your life, and we hope we can influence you to follow Christ and see Him as the giver of every good and perfect gift, including recovery. That's part of who we are, Rob.

ROB: So, that began in the fall of 2014. I recognize you have had phenomenal growth. What do the statistics look like today?

RANDY: I'm proud to share this with you. We are presently at forty chapters in Indiana, five chapters in Ohio, one in Virginia, and one in South Carolina. The chapter in South Carolina is only minutes from Myrtle Beach. I'd like to visit that one more often, especially in the winter. We're in twenty-seven Indiana counties, three Ohio counties, one in Virginia, and one in South Carolina. We have a total attendance of somewhere around 900-1,000. Pre-Covid, we were at a little over 1,100 members. We have been able to assist—both with finances and support—over 1,800 individuals in getting treatment. Currently, we have at least eighty former and present attendees that have found employment in the recovery field. We are very proud of that. We have had over 750 people commit or recommit to Christ through our faith-based effort. We have spoken to over 27,000 students in grades K-12. I can give you the names of eight to ten recovery groups and organizations that have reported to us that they modeled themselves after our design.

ROB: These groups have been birthed out of what you're doing, as well?

RANDY: Yes, they spawned from us.

ROB: That's wonderful.

Randy: It's the old idea of "imitation is the best form of flattery." We accept that, and we count their success as a part of our success. We are involved in seventeen or eighteen different denominations. None of that is little—and I don't want to demean it in any way—but what is most exciting for us right now, is what we're doing right here, our *Faith In Your Recovery* podcast. It is available on all major podcast platforms, and a new episode airs each Friday. We continue to state that we're about all things recovery. That means we interview guests from the medical and healthcare fields, those that have struggled with addiction, family members of strugglers, law enforcement personnel, community leaders, members of multiple recovery groups, and others. We want to interview anybody who's been touched in any way by addiction. Our number-one-listened-to podcast is an interview with a gentleman by the name of Dan Watson. Dan is the former mayor of Dunkirk, Indiana. His son, Justin, died of an overdose. His story will knock your socks off. More good news for our podcast is that on January 8, 2023, it was picked up by MIX 105 Internet Radio. It is available Sunday mornings, bright and early at 5:30 a.m. But if you're listening in London, that's not all bad. MIX 105 has a lot of listeners there.

ROB: Because it's all over the world.

RANDY: Yeah, and it is also available on Sunday mornings at 7:45, on our local station in Portland, Indiana, WPGW Radio 100.9. They do our podcast as a part of their worship lineup. What's neat about that is listeners who will never attend a meeting or listen to a podcast are starting to understand the struggle. This allows us to effectively break the bias and stop the stigma associated with addiction.

ROB: Yeah, there's a lot of power in that podcast. Unfortunately, you hear a person's story, you hear their journey, and you might think, "Well, you know, I'm somehow better than they are." Then you hear their experiences and struggles, and you realize the validity of their stories and the realities of their lives. Finally, understanding settles in and it changes the way you view their lives and struggles. I've always believed in the idea that we need to put things on a shelf that everyone can reach. And I believe the podcast puts the recovery conversations and understanding of people in recovery on a shelf that everyone can reach. And that's the power of this program.

RANDY: Earlier Rob, you mentioned adverse childhood experiences. In one of our episodes, we talked with Kali, who at the age of nine was introduced to drugs by her babysitter. You know it was nothing she would have chosen at that age. Why wouldn't she have thought it was OK? It was coming from the babysitter, someone that you trust to care for you. And there are many other stories where it was an innocent thing. In one of our recent interviews, a young man shared with us how during his military time in Iraq, an IED exploded beneath his hummer and the shrapnel damaged his foot and leg. That explosion placed him in the hospital for thirteen months on an IV pain drip. Any questions about why he came out of the hospital seeking drugs? He started with prescription drugs and moved progressively to harder street drugs and everything that followed. Not everybody is out there hunting for a high. Some just don't know how to let go of the moment they've found themselves in. I have one final thought for now concerning our podcast; a note that we are excited about and thankful for. We think it gives validity to who we are. In November 2022, PODSTATUS (podstatus.com) reported to us that among all not-for-profit podcasts on the Apple platform, which is #1 as far as platforms in the entire United States, we were ranked #53.

ROB: That's amazing! That's incredible news!

RANDY: If I had hair, it would curl. That's all there is to it. These kinds of results excite an old guy like me. This is God at work in recovery.

ROB: Which is just more of a reminder that what you're doing matters. It has hit a cord with the listener and makes a difference.

RANDY: Rob, I'll tell you, I'm a man of faith, and I've seen God work in this in ways I've never seen him work before in my ministry or my life. His ways are just so far beyond mine; His vision is so much better. He sees it. He shows us the path and we're doing our best to follow it. He is the reason we have gotten this far.

ROB: Yeah, and you know, another reminder is that God doesn't waste any of this. He uses these things to help others, and He's using Brianna's tragedy to touch the lives of so many others. As I recall, you mentioned earlier that there were more than 1,700 people in treatment through this program. And to think that that's more than how many people live in your entire hometown. That is so powerful.

RANDY: Yes, that's just like, "Pick up the whole town and move them to the rehab."

ROB: That's right. So, if I'm a listener and I want more information—maybe I want to know how to get a chapter of A Better Life - Brianna's Hope in my community, or in my church, or my civic group, or wherever—how would I go about doing that?

RANDY: Thank you for asking that. Number one, if you have further interest in who we are and what we're about, go to our website: ablbh.org. Our website is simply the initials for A Better Life - Brianna's Hope. There is a drop-down menu that you can click that will explain how to open a chapter in your community. Please understand that we don't care where you are located. You don't have to be in Indiana. As we have already shared, we are in three other states. That means a presence in four states which leaves us with forty-six to go. We would love to help you make one happen close to you. Have your church, group, club, or organization contact us, and we will arrange a time and place to come and do training. For more information, email us at info@ablbh.org. After we speak, if you're still interested, we will come to you and do a training session for three to three-and-a-half hours. We will share some SWAG (free promotional items) with you and then, with a little bit of help and some other gifts and support, you will be ready to open your chapter and get things rolling toward recovery in your community. Understand, one of our unique selling points is that we are not a twelve-step program. We have no issue with twelve-step programs, and in many ways, we overlap. We use some of those steps, but that is not who we are. We have our own design. Some people have found that refreshing and helpful. Some are not ready for the rigid rules, and some are. We get that. We won't interfere with your choice to float from one to the other. We are an "other choice" as it says in Brianna's prayer. Finally, if you have questions about the podcast, you can reach us at podcast@ablbh.org. We'd love to hear from you.

ROB: Great. That's excellent. What if somebody wanted to support you financially?

RANDY: PayPal is readily accessed on our website. Should you choose to send a check, our address is also there. Give our office a call if you're wanting to give, have any questions, or want to find out more. The website also has our phone number. Should you wonder, we are a 501(c)(3), which allows you that tax deduction for charitable gifts.

ROB: So, you've been around for eight years now?

RANDY: Yes.

ROB: You've had extraordinary growth. I listened to an earlier podcast—maybe from a little over a year ago—and you were at thirty-seven chapters. You have grown quite a bit in the last year. Additionally, the podcast has a wonderful outreach as well. I am guessing that hasn't been easy.

RANDY: Right. The Covid pandemic made it quite challenging for our meetings and our strugglers. We had to go to remote meetings and that limited growth, simply because of the social distancing. Isolation for someone battling addiction can be deadly. But God has more than blessed us financially. As with most costs, ours are continuing to climb. We continue to help strugglers get into rehab. We have peer recovery coaches we can bring on board to assist. If you will own it, and you're sincere, we will work hard to give you the chance for recovery. We want to be here for you and with you.

ROB: That's awesome. In one of the earlier episodes, you said that you often felt like a boomerang and that you refused to be thrown away. You said you would keep coming back. I like that point because that is what I have seen from ABLBH over the last few years. Covid shut down so many things, but you would not let that shut you down.

RANDY: That has always been my attitude in life. I'm not going to give up on an individual because of their struggles, though there may be moments I have to step away and then come back to them. It reminds me of the scripture passage where Jesus tells the disciples to go into the city, and if they are not welcome, they should shake the dust off their feet and leave. I will give up on you when Jesus does, which is never. We must guard against enabling the struggler because it usually hurts more than it helps.

ROB: Right, because that is what it requires; total tenacity and commitment. It is that continuing to show up and the desire to keep bouncing back.

RANDY: That's it. You're going to find out that in recovery, most will experience some type of relapse while on the journey. All of us experience relapses. We relapse in our behaviors, be it with our spouse, our children, or our parents. We relapse while on a diet, and that may not be as deadly as something that might contain fentanyl, but we all have our relapse moments. I think of the constant stumbling of Peter as recorded in the scriptures. We have to accept people where they are and as they are. We don't have to like it, and we can pray for God to change them, but seldom will we. Caution: We all have another relapse in us, but we don't know if we have another recovery.

ROB: Earlier, when I asked you for your bio, you told me how you got to where you are, but what if you weren't doing this? For example, I went to school to be a finance guy. Addiction touched my life via relatives and family members, but I've never been a recovery guy. I've never been engaged in that. And yet, God sort of navigated me out of being a chief financial officer into running a homeless shelter, a sober living facility, and all the other services that we do. I guess we never know where God's going to lead us next. So, if you weren't doing this, what would you be doing?

RANDY: I honestly don't know what I'd be doing if it wasn't for this and continued ministry. By nature, I have always been a people person. I had the good fortune years ago of announcing several sports at the local high school and coaching middle school football and wrestling. I also did a lot of substitute teaching. If I had not been called into ministry in my earlier years, I would have wanted to have been a teacher at the middle school level. I love that age group. I would find a way to be involved with them today if I wasn't doing this. That's one of the joys of ABLBH. We get to go into the schools and speak. It is so meaningful and validating to know that you are impacting the lives of our youth. When we do a convocation, we take three or four individuals along who have been there, done that, and have the scars to prove it. As they tell their stories, you see heads shake and chins drop.

ROB: During this interview two words keep coming up. Those two words are faith and hope. Hope has its reasons, doesn't it?

RANDY: Absolutely. Yes. I believe a ray of hope is strong enough to lead us to the Light that can show us the way out of the darkness. And faith becomes your hope and that's the way you're sometimes able to climb out of that hole.

ROB: Yeah. There's something that's so forward-looking, in an encouraging manner, that hope provides us, and I love that. And I love the fact it constantly pops up in this interview so often.

RANDY: The author, Hal Lindsey, is often quoted as saying, "Man can live about forty days without food, about three days without water, about eight minutes without air, but only for one second without hope." Deprive someone of hope and life has little reason or purpose.

ROB: Right, that's beautiful. Randy, this has been a real pleasure. You normally end your podcast with this: The name of this podcast is *Faith In Your Recovery*. What do these four words mean to you?

RANDY: I've used that question more times than I've answered it.

ROB: Right. So, you said we were going to turn the tables, so there you go.

RANDY: Absolutely. I respect that. *Faith In Your Recovery* means this to me: you are not going to do it on your own. It takes more than a village, more than your family, more than your friends. It takes all of that together, but at the head of it all needs to be God. Place God first and the rest will be easier. Please, don't misunderstand me, I didn't say *easy*. I said, *easier*. You will have a strength above and beyond your own that you could not build at the gym or in your head or heart. *Faith In Your Recovery* also requires faith in yourself, faith in God, faith in those around you, and faith in your future.

ROB: Yeah, that's beautiful. I love that. Randy, thank you for the impact that you and this podcast have had on the recovery community and for helping us all learn more about what's going on in the world of addiction and recovery. Thank you for having me and giving me the honor of participating in this conversation with you. Thanks, and God bless you, my friend.

RANDY: And thank you, Rob. Thank you for your willingness to be involved. And folks, don't hesitate to contact us. We want to hear from you, as we want to continue to impact the lives of those who are struggling and those who are affected by that struggle. We care. We can prove it. You hang in there. Don't give up. Your answer may be just around the corner, who knows, it may be in our next episode of *Faith In Your Recovery*. God bless. Amen.

Order of an ABLBH Support & Recovery Meeting

1. Welcome & Announcements (12 minutes)
   a) Reading/Poem/Positive scripture
   b) Word from Team Hope
   c) Announcements
      i. Information for the evening
      ii. Review of Past Week
   d) What's Happening?
   e) Save A Friend
   f) Brianna's Prayer shared out loud at every meeting.
2. Victories and Struggles Reports & Presentation of Victory Tags (10-12 minutes)
3. Mini-Lesson (15 minutes)
4. Break (10 minutes)
5. Lesson or sharing by someone that has "Been There, Done That, and Has the Scars to Prove It" (25-30 minutes)
6. Closing Remarks and Words of Inspiration (10 minutes)
7. Prayer

Please remember:
  † You have agreed to follow this standard order of meeting as have all other chapters to preserve conformity among chapters, giving communities a stronger sense of who we are.
  † We need this to maintain our integrity and identification as connected and united chapters of ABLBH.
  † We encourage you to add to this standard order to make it your own without straying outside of it.

Brianna's Prayer

"Please Lord, look after me and my family. Please help me to do the right thing and to show people I'm not a bad person inside or out and help me Lord to get through this disappointment again and know I make mistakes but who doesn't? I don't do it to do wrong. I do it cuz I feel I have no other choice. I want a better life, Lord, I do. Please help me. Do to me as what you feel is best. I surrender to you. In Jesus' name, Amen."

Chapter Two

Dan Watson – "If I'd only known."

"And the God of all grace, who called you to his eternal glory in Christ, after you have suffered a little while, will himself restore you and make you strong, firm and steadfast."
(1 Pet. 5:10 NIV)

On the morning of August 22, 2017, thirty-year-old Justin Watson was found unresponsive in his hotel room in Cincinnati, Ohio. Medical examiners concluded that Justin died from an overdose of the drug fentanyl. Justin came from a close-knit family and was survived by his father, mother, sister, brother, girlfriend, and newborn son. His family has suffered unimaginable grief, and they are still trying to make sense of some of his choices in life and how drug addiction ultimately led to his untimely death.

Justin's younger sister, Jessica, also struggles with addiction. She has been in and out of jail over the last twenty years for various drug-related charges. Her family desperately wants to help her win her battle against drugs.

Dan Watson is their father. He and his wife, Kelly, understand the hurt, struggle, anger, and pain of losing a child. Dan has also experienced the frustration of trying to help a child that isn't ready for help. On August 1, 2022, Dan shared his story on the *Faith In Your Recovery* podcast, which marked the first time he spoke publicly about his experience, nearly five years after Justin's death. Dan agreed to this interview with the hope that his story could help other parents of children struggling with addiction know that they are not alone.

RANDY: I have a special guest with me today and his name is Dan Watson. I'd like for you to begin by telling us about some of your life experiences and a little bit of your professional resume.

DAN: OK, I was raised mostly in Dunkirk, Indiana. My mom and dad moved to Delaware County in 1967. I graduated from Delta High School and went to college at Tri-State University in Angola, where I got my Bachelor of Science degree in civil engineering. After college, I worked for five years for the Indiana Department of Transportation, in downtown Indianapolis. Then, I had the opportunity to go back to Jay County. One of the county commissioners at that time was a good friend of mine and talked me into coming back. In 1989, I took the job as a county engineer and held that position until I retired in December of last year. Now, I work for a private engineering firm in Indianapolis, and I'm just having a ball. Also, I've been involved in the government. I spent nine years on the city council in Dunkirk, and four years as mayor. I'm currently on the board that works with Mayor Jack Robbins.

RANDY: Today, Dan is going to share with us some of his family experiences and the losses and the challenges that he's been through. As I reflect, I think our first real connection was when I coached your son, Justin, in football at West Jay Middle School. I had him for seventh and eighth-grade football. You're a father of three, right? Would you introduce us to your three kids, please?

DAN: Yes. Justin was the oldest and then I have a daughter, Jessica. She is thirty-one, and I have a son, Jaiden, who just turned sixteen in the summer.

RANDY: Well, in a moment we are going to dig in just a little bit deeper into some of those experiences, and I thought the way we might do that is to begin by just having you speak about each one of your kids individually. What has been special about them? What's made them unique; their challenges, struggles, and victories as life has played out? So, Dan, just go ahead if you want and start us off with a little of Justin's story, OK?

DAN: OK. Justin was a smart kid. He always got good grades in school. He played football and basketball. I coached him in little league. He played little league, and I was very involved. I think he didn't really know what he wanted to do when he got out

30

of school, so he ended up enlisting in the Army. I think it was a good fit for him because he needed direction. He did well in the Army. I think the proudest day of my life was when he graduated from basic training, and we went out to that ceremony. I was really proud. It was a proud day.

RANDY: Where was that Dan?

DAN: His basic training was in South Carolina, but he ended up being stationed in Missouri. When he got out of the Army, he came home and wasn't sure what he wanted to do. He had a few odd jobs here and there, and then he took to working as a millwright. He really liked it. He learned how to weld and do all that kind of stuff. We thought he found his way. He met a girl, Lindsey Cochran, and they got together. I think the proudest day of *his* life was when his son, Jameson, was born. His son is four years old now. Justin passed away on August 22, 2017. That was two weeks after his son was born, and a week before his thirty-first birthday. So, it went from being one of the proudest days of my life to one of the hardest days of my life.

RANDY: Unimaginable. I can't... you know, there's no way I can say I know what you're thinking or what you're feeling because I haven't been there.

DAN: Jessica is my second child. She's very smart and very athletic. Jess played softball, basketball... you name it. She did all that. She got a scholarship to go to Ball State, and then she just fell into the whole addiction thing. She has probably spent most of the last ten years in and out of jail. It's been hard. Jaiden is my youngest. He's completely different from Justin and Jessica. He's very smart, but he keeps to himself more. He's not as social, and he doesn't play sports. Evidently, God knew what he was doing when he gave Kelly and me Jaiden that late in our life, because I don't know what we would do without him. He's just been a blessing.

RANDY: That's awesome. Please, tell us a little bit more about some of the first visuals or ideas you had recognizing Justin was headed in the direction of addiction.

DAN: You know, I didn't. I don't think I saw it as much with Justin as I did with Jess. I knew that he was using. I knew he had some issues, but I didn't see that it was an addiction. I didn't think that he had the problem as bad as Jessica did. Of course, he wasn't home much because he was in the Army. He wasn't living at home, so I guess I didn't see it as much as I did with Jess. I didn't really know where his mind was. I have a letter. Justin wrote everything down. He constantly kept a journal. If you don't mind, I'll just read it.

RANDY: We'd love it.

DAN: It will give you an idea of what his mindset was. This was written on August 11th, so it would have been right after his son was born and just before he passed away. So, I will just read it, and it will kind of give you a feel for his priorities and what he was thinking and feeling at that time.

"It still blows my mind that I'm a father. I have a son. I never thought that my entire world, along with any and every single little thought or feeling of importance could be wrapped up in one little, tiny guy. It makes me melt every time those blue eyes open and look up at me. I know in my heart and soul that I'll never fail him. I will always stand behind him, even if he's wrong. It's my job—no, it is my honor—to be a father to that amazing little boy. It's just as much an honor that I've been given the chance over the past three and a half years to be a father figure to Lilly. She really is awesome and will in no doubt succeed in her lifetime. I know this because her mother instilled the wisdom and the fight she needs. I just hope I can impact that boy's life the same and give him every piece of knowledge I possibly can as well as any other tool he might need in life. That is what my old man, my hero, my dad, gave me. He gave me so much more than that. He devoted everything he had into making life for Jess and me easier, or at the very least, bearable. Mom wasn't absent in all this either. She was Dad's teammate and together they did more than right by Jess and me. Now they have the chance to do it again with Jaiden. The one thing that still stumps me is how Jess ended up in prison for the better part of her twenties and how I ended up turning into the dirtbag heroin addict that I was. I'm so relieved to have left that part of me behind. I never once thought I could ever become someone so ugly inside and out. It took a long time and a journey down a painful road, but it definitely helped shape me into someone much stronger than I was before. That's why I don't stress as much about my issue now. I know that I can and will overcome it in the end. And in all reality, the end should have been August 6th, the day my son was born. For five days, everything was perfect. I didn't have any thoughts or cravings. Then again, I never really do. I think it has to have control over me for that type of mental state to be present. For the time being, I remain in control. I'm just trying to break the habit before the tables turn and I succumb to the emptiness and the darkness overwhelms me. I'm starting to think that maybe my quarrel with the Big Guns upstairs should be resolved. I think I've kept a grudge long enough. Not to mention, the sins I've been piling up could really use several confession sessions. I just hope I can say enough "Hail Marys" and "Our Father" prayers to lessen the load. I actually remember not ever wanting to get up and go to church, but I always felt better after going. I mean like my complete heart, mind, body, and soul felt better. I think I need some churchin' 'cause I've been sinnin'. Sunday, August 13th at St. Mary's is where I'm going to be. I still remember mass starts at 10:30 sharp. I already feel better. Got to go. Little sister is coming for some of my Army uniform patches and the first challenge coin I ever earned that I usually have on me at all times. It is going to be a great night."

DAN: That was written just eleven days before he passed away.

RANDY: So, did you find that letter? Was it given to you before that? How did you come across that letter? Because that's gold.

DAN: They found it when they found him. Justin went to Cincinnati. He was going to start a new job. He had driven down the day before and had to do a drug screen. He passed his drug screen, and he was supposed to start that next morning, August 22nd. I remember trying to call him that morning to wish him luck on his first day. It was probably 10:30 or 11:00 that morning that the sheriff, Dwayne Ford, came into my office at the highway garage and said, "We found Justin." That's when he told me, and I just—ooh, that was rough. I said, "What do you mean they found him?" The sheriff answered, "Well they found him in his hotel room." He had OD'd, and this letter was found with all his things. He had it with him. He had kept a journal. After reading that letter, I kind of thought, "He knew that he had a problem, and he was going to fight this thing." I don't know what happened. I have no clue. We still don't know. We just know that he died of a fentanyl overdose. That's what the report said. So, yeah, it was rough. It still is. It's hard.

RANDY: You don't quickly get over that kind of pain, and I don't know for sure if you ever completely get over it.

DAN: No, I don't think so.

RANDY: Hopefully, time will lessen some of it, but that kind of tragic loss hangs with you. In the letter, there's a statement I picked up on. He referred to himself as a "dirtbag addict." Did you ever feel that toward him?

DAN: No, not at all.

RANDY: What did you feel toward him, even amidst the struggle?

DAN: He was my son. Addiction is a struggle. I understand that now more than ever. I smoke cigarettes and that's an addiction. Somehow, addictions can just get a hold of you. I think you get to where you'll do anything. Justin obviously had the birth of his son in his mind, and if that doesn't change you—if that's not even enough to change you—I don't know. The feeling that you get when reading his letter is that you fall into this emptiness. I don't know that feeling, and I guess unless you're an addict, you probably don't.

RANDY: There's no way I could. I hear it. I listen to it. I understand it. But I've certainly not lived it. There's that desperation to get away from it, and yet it just pulls you back so strongly, and it sucks you in so much deeper each time. How did you and Kelly approach things amidst his addiction struggles? What was your plan?

DAN: Well, he had talked to his mother about getting help, and we were going to help him. We said we would do whatever it took because he wanted to go get help. I thought he had it under control, and when he was ready, he would go. That day obviously never came. But the signs were there. I see them all the time. I see them with Jessica all the time.

RANDY: Has your hindsight with Justin's experience helped you see Jess's challenges more clearly?

DAN: Probably, but Jess had issues before. I think she had issues way before Justin did. I think she started with the people she hung out with. The drugs were there, and I think she got involved when she was just out of high school, or maybe when she was still in high school. She got into trouble. I think her first jail time was for dealing. There was an informant that was supposedly a friend of hers that she sold a couple of pills to. That ended up costing her. I think they sentenced her to twelve years, reduced it to eight, and she had to do four. She did that and then had to go back to prison. She's currently sitting in the Jay County Jail right now.

RANDY: Amidst this, and prior to Justin's death, what do you think was the hardest thing for you and Kelly?

DAN: It's knowing that we couldn't do anything. I used to think it was a stigma, but I hear people talk about how it is poor people that get addicted and it's not well-to-do people. I'm not saying we're well-to-do, by any means, but our kids never needed anything. We took care of our kids. They had whatever they needed. They had a good education. We raised them the right way. I don't know where we went wrong. I feel like maybe if there's one thing that we regret now, it's "What did we do wrong?" and we don't know. You just keep thinking, "What could we have done differently? What could we have done differently?" and I just don't know what we could have done differently.

RANDY: If you'd have known, you'd have done it, right? If you'd have thought, "I know what is going to work," you'd have left work to get it done. I know you that well, and I know how much you love your kids and your family. At Justin's passing, where were you guys relationally? Were you in a good place? Some families aren't in the end.

DAN: We were. Everybody was. It was an exciting time. He'd just had a baby, and everybody was excited, and he was getting ready to start a new job. I don't know if it was that all those things were just too overwhelming. I just don't know. I don't know what caused him to do it that one last time, but I think we were all in a good place.

RANDY: You referred to being filled with "would've, could've, should've," but we don't know what they are. How have you guys managed to heal to this point? I'm not suggesting you're totally healed. I know better, but what has gotten you through to this point as you've dealt with the passing of Justin and with Jessica's challenges and addiction issues?

DAN: Probably Jaiden. Like I said, he's been such a blessing. Also, our two grandbabies. We've got Justin's and then we've got Jess's. We watch Jess's baby between two and four days a week, and Kelly is watching Jameson, Justin's son, every day so Lindsey can go back to work. Kelly retired in July so she can spend time with the grandkids. That, I think, helps get us through, because when we see Jameson, we see Justin. They're so much alike. And the same way with Jess. I think the hardest thing with Jess is her denial. One thing I've noticed with most addicts, and the feelings they've shared in situations we've had, is that they're always in denial, and they will never admit that they're using. They say, "No, that's not mine. No, I didn't do that. No, no, no." One thing Kelly and I know, just being around Jess her whole life, is when she's on something, and when she's using. She will deny it every time, no matter what. You could find it or find her with a needle stuck in her arm, and she'd say, "That's not mine; I didn't put that there." We've tried to help Jess. We've taken her to different places. She gets past the first day or two and gets to where she's feeling a bit better, and then she'll leave. You can't force them to go. Obviously, she's thirty years old, and she can do whatever she wants. All you can do is try to encourage them to go, but it's not until they admit they have a problem. And if they're still in denial and they will not admit they have a problem, I don't think it will change.

RANDY: They have to own it.

DAN: They have to, and you know we'll do anything for her, but getting someone to admit they have a problem is the first step. And we just can't get to that point with Jess. I mean, it's hard.

The Recovery Village addresses how to approach denial:

"No matter what the person's behavior has been like, it's important to remember that your loved one is not a bad person; he or she has an addiction and is in deep denial. Addiction can cause our loved ones to act in negative ways and cause hurt to those around them. It may be difficult, but it's important not to blame or criticize them.

- Be specific when you talk. Bring up specific incidents that they know about and have participated in like canceled plans or broken promises.
- Use "I" phrases such as, "I was worried," or, "I noticed."
- Talk about the negative effects your loved one's using has on the things he or she cares about most, such as their career, family, sports, or other commitments.

Continued...

- Don't be discouraged or surprised if your loved one continues to deny they have a problem. Unfortunately, denial is one of the symptoms of the disease of addiction. Don't take it personally and remain supportive of your loved one.
- Keep in touch with your loved one even if they aren't open to help right now. You never know when you may have planted the seed of recovery."

(The Recovery Village. n.d. "How to Help Someone in Denial of Their Addiction." Accessed April 3, 2023, https://www.therecoveryvillage.com/family-friend-portal/how-to-help-someone-in-denial-of-their-addiction)

RANDY: Going back again to Justin's statement where he called himself a dirtbag addict, did you ever feel like people looked down on him or you guys because of his addiction issue, or that it was what defined his life, or even Jess's life?

DAN: I don't think so with him because I don't think there are many people that knew that he had a problem. On the other hand, with Jessica, pretty much everybody is aware of it. I think ten years ago it would have been that way. I don't think it's that way anymore. I know so many people that have had the same problem. They have gone through it. They've faced the same thing, and they're good kids. They were brought up right. They just fell into this addiction.

RANDY: They made bad choices.

DAN: I don't know what the answer is. I know everybody is trying. Probably the one thing I feel bad about is that I really want to get involved in programs like Brianna's Hope, but my feeling is, "How am I going to be able to help anybody when I was not even able to help my own son?" Do you know what I mean?

RANDY: I hear what you're saying, but you have a knowledge and an understanding that most people do not have, because you have been there and done that, and you're feeling the scars of your children's choices. What you're doing here today, by letting people know what your experience was about, is going to give them an opportunity to release some of their feelings, and say, "Somebody gets it." You're somebody who gets it. You may not be able to help that struggler, but you may help the struggler's parents more than you realize. I can certainly see the positivity in that. That leads to this thought: Do you feel like you have had the freedom from those in the community to talk about Justin's life, and about Jess in a positive way? Or do you feel like you've had to, kind of, hold it in?

DAN: Not really. We don't hold it in. I mean, it is what it is. If people accept it, fine. If they don't accept it, fine. There's nothing I can do, and there's nothing Kelly can do to change what happened. I think we have enough friends around that understand what we went through, and that helps us a lot as we're getting through it. There are so many kids that Justin and Jess grew up with that have been through this. It has happened to other people, so it's not just us. I think that's what we realize. This is not just an isolated incident. This is a crisis, and it affects everybody. You know, Jay County is not a big county, but you can hardly find anybody that has not been affected directly by this.

RANDY: When I go to a church, club, group, or organization to speak, I usually open with the question: "How many of you have a family member or know someone that struggles with addiction?" And the hands that don't go up need to move the rock they're living under because we've all been impacted by it exactly as you're saying here. So, from your experiences, what would you like for others that might be walking in your shoes to know? Or what kind of advice might you be able to give them, Dan?

DAN: First, I don't think you can judge them, because like I said, I think it's just beyond our control. You have to try to help them all you can, but there again, you can only do so much if they aren't willing to get the help. Also, you don't know what it's like. None of us knows what it's like if we haven't been there. All you can do is be there for your kids. Try to help them all you can. You know, if you have questions or you think your kid might be involved in drugs, chances are *they are*! If you see any signs or have any doubts, they probably are using drugs.

RANDY: I would think you would be better off taking for granted they are and being wrong than finding out the other way that you could have been right. So, yes, yes.

DAN: And we have gone from not just cocaine and heroin and meth to this fentanyl that they're putting in everything that will kill you. It blows my mind that it's just taken over like it has. It seems like addicts would think, "Gosh, I can't do this anymore because there's a chance I could get some of this bad stuff." But they don't think past that next high to realize what the outcome could be. It's a scary thing.

> "Most recent cases of fentanyl-related overdose are linked to illicitly manufactured fentanyl, which is distributed through illegal drug markets for its heroin-like effect. It is often added to other drugs because of its extreme potency, which makes drugs cheaper, more powerful, more addictive, and more dangerous. Powdered fentanyl looks just like many other drugs. It is commonly mixed with drugs like heroin, cocaine, and methamphetamine and made into pills that are made to resemble other prescription opioids. Fentanyl-laced drugs are extremely dangerous, and many people may be unaware that their drugs are laced with fentanyl."
>
> (Centers for Disease Control and Prevention. n.d. "Fentanyl Facts." accessed April 3, 2023, https://www.cdc.gov/stopoverdose/fentanyl/index.html)

RANDY: So, can you think of anything else you'd like to address as you help others by sharing all this, Dan?

DAN: I don't know. I guess I realize that I'm not alone. I know there are a lot of people out there that are going through the same thing, and there are a lot more that are going to go through the same thing because this isn't going to stop overnight. I think one of the biggest issues—and I know they're trying to work on it—is trying to get more local treatment. We have to send our kids off to Fort Wayne or Indianapolis, and if we had a local facility, maybe it would help. I know there's been a lot of talk of doing something like that, but these kids hear the horror stories from the people that have been to those places, and it doesn't make them want to go. I think a facility that welcomes people—welcomes addicts in—and actually works with the addicts would help. Also, I think we're wasting our time when the court orders these addicts to go to treatment. After all, they're going because they're forced to go, and you're trying to force somebody to do something they don't want to do. My feeling is that the only way the treatment is going to work is if the addict decides it's time. When they think, "I want to do this," and then they go for the treatment. I wish I knew what the answer was. I really do.

RANDY: If we did, we wouldn't be here today, would we? And, unfortunately, the struggle is becoming greater.

DAN: I know. It's scary to think how many of them are out there. They have just got to realize that they're not alone either, but there again, do they feel that way? Like Justin, he felt like he was alone. His letter said the way he felt, and I hate to think that the kids that are using drugs feel that way. I understand they made a bad choice and it's not just as easy as, "OK, I made a bad choice. I'm not going to do that anymore." With these drugs, it's an addiction, so they need help.

RANDY: Yes, and there is danger. It can be one-and-done, unfortunately. There's no such thing as experimenting with drugs today. Well Dan, is there anything else you'd like to say?

DAN: I don't know. This is the first time I've really talked to anybody about this. So, it's kind of new to me and I wasn't sure how I was going to be prepared for this, so if it helps, it helps. I mean, it's all we can try to do.

RANDY: And you have tried. Thank you for making yourself vulnerable like this; for making your family vulnerable, and for speaking the truth. For you to step up here and share this will definitely touch lives, and I believe even change and save lives.

DAN: I hope.

Since this interview was recorded, Jessica Watson has been released from jail and is working diligently on her recovery. Jaiden Watson continues to do well in high school. Dan and Kelly Watson love spending time with their grandbabies and each other.

Chapter 3

Lindsey Cochran– "Not again, God. Not again"

"Look carefully then how you walk, not as unwise but as wise." (Eph. 5:15 NIV) Lindsey is the mother of two. She first met her husband-to-be, Daniel, while in third grade. Years later, they were married and had their daughter, Lilly. The marriage had highs and lows, but ended in divorce, largely due to Daniel's substance abuse disorder.

After the divorce, Lindsey met Justin Watson. They fell in love and had a son named Jameson together. Two weeks after his birth, on August 22, 2017, Justin died of an overdose.

Daniel, Lindsey's ex-husband, entered a period of sobriety after Justin died, and he would often help Lindsey with Lilly and Jameson. He became a real friend to her again. Tragically, on November 3, 2018, Daniel also died of a drug overdose. Both of Lindsey's children were left without fathers.

Despite all odds, Lindsey has come through this double tragedy with determination to provide her children with a wonderful life and a will to help others in similar situations.

RANDY: We have a guest with us. We want to welcome you, Lindsey.

LINDSEY: Thank you for having me, Randy.

RANDY: It's a joy to have you with us. We appreciate your willingness to share. Lindsey, tell the folks who you are and what you're doing in life right now.

LINDSEY: OK. My name is Lindsey Rogers. I'm a mother of two. I work at the Commercial Review. I sell advertising.

RANDY: How long have you been working at the Commercial Review?

LINDSEY: I worked there for ten years, and then I took a little break for a few years, and I've been back since September.

RANDY: The Commercial Review is the Jay County paper published here in Portland, Indiana. And Lindsey has been a part of that for quite some time, working in the advertising department. Lindsey, what kind of personal interests do you have—hobbies, dreams, hopes—right now?

LINDSEY: I listen to a lot of music, and I do yoga at night. I also do a lot of meditation. I guess if I had a dream, it would be to help the children of addicts. I feel like we spend a lot of time helping addicts, but the children need help too.

RANDY: We're going to find out why you have such an affinity for that, due to some of your life experiences, and your own daughter and son, and the effects of what addiction has done to their lives. Tell us about your early childhood.

LINDSEY: I grew up in Redkey, Indiana. My parents were the most loving, wonderful people I could ever hope for or dream of. I had a brother named Matt, who was a wonderful big brother. We had a neighborhood full of kids. In high school, I was a cheerleader. I had a lot of friends. I think I was a happy-go-lucky person. I played softball and just tried to have fun. I had a lot of fun.

RANDY: Will you share with us how you and your husband, Daniel, connected?

LINDSEY: I met Daniel in third grade. He had moved to Redkey with his father, and it was love at first sight. He was funny. He was cute. And he had a real charisma about him. For the next several years, it was like a cat-and-mouse game with him chasing me, and I just wasn't quite ready to have a boyfriend. Finally, in our senior year, we started dating, and we were together for a lot of years after that.

RANDY: He was also very athletic. I can remember his skills in junior high and high school, especially in football. He didn't back down from much of anything, and he'd take it on. So, Lindsey, let's go ahead and move on from high school. The relationship began officially with dating and that led to marriage. Tell us about Daniel.

LINDSEY: Ah, Daniel was an amazing person. He was so full of life and fun. He was a go-getter and a good provider for the family. He was in the military for a while, and he really excelled at that.

RANDY: What branch of the military was he in?

LINDSEY: He was in the Marines. Then, we were both in college. I was going to Indiana University. He was in Terre Haute, going to Indiana State University. We would visit on the weekends a lot and we realized we didn't like to be apart. So, we decided to come home and go to school where we could be a little closer. It seemed like we were always missing school because one of us was always visiting the other. So, we came back home to Redkey. I went to Ball State, and he got accepted into the electricians' union. Life was good then.

RANDY: I can remember Daniel showing me his journeyman's card. He was an extremely young journeyman electrician. I want to say he was like twenty-four. Is that pretty close?

LINDSEY: Yes.

RANDY: To have his journeyman's card at that age—if you know anything about the process—that says a bunch about who he was. We would talk about that at times, and as you said, Daniel excelled at a lot of things. But I know Daniel then started to have some struggles and challenges. He got into those areas that just started to darken his life. Tell us about that.

LINDSEY: Well, at one point we split up, and I think he kind of got stuck in Redkey. I think it's kind of what you did back then. There wasn't a lot to do in Redkey, and on the weekends I think kids would just get together and they would party and have fun. I remember, at one point, he would call himself a "weekend warrior." It was where he could just do things on the weekends. And then during the week, he would go to work.

RANDY: He could function during the week. I was speaking with someone the other day, and they said, "That's just how it was. It's who we were. It's how we rolled. That was our life during that time." We have mentioned the town of Redkey, but it's not unique in that respect. It happens in most small towns, and even larger towns, within given districts.

LINDSEY: We had split up. I was living in Muncie, and he was living at home. Then some bad things happened in his life—nothing drug related—and I decided to go check on him and see how he was. When I did, it was back to love at first sight, I guess, and we got back together. But he had a drug problem at that time that I did not know was serious. I thought, "Well, he loves me. He wants to be with me. It's something he'll just quit now." That's just how I thought it worked. As time went on, I realized it was a bigger issue than I had anticipated, and that he wasn't just going to quit.

RANDY: Had he, at that point, been able to face and admit and label his battle, his fight, his addiction? Was he still in denial?

LINDSEY: He was still in denial. He thought he was just having fun.

RANDY: Did he think he could control it instead of it controlling him?

LINDSEY: Yes.

RANDY: He thought he could battle that and win. He could play on the weekends and get real during the week. I'm going to guess that it started to change from two-day weekends to three-day, to four-day, and then it started to take over.

LINDSEY: Yes. I was in school at the time. We lived in a little house that we rented. He was in the electrician's union, and he started missing classes for the union. Thank God he always tended to put responsibility first, so when he would see he was going off track, he would kind of focus back on work. It just got to the point where Daniel was a full-time responsibility. I think I kind of took it on my own shoulders. It felt like I was trying to save a life at that time. Eventually, it became so much that I quit school, and he was all I could focus on. It had just spiraled so far out of control that it was like he wasn't in there anymore. I was trying to hold on to him. He was falling down this huge hole, and I was just trying to hold on for him.

RANDY: You were his lifeline at that time. The way you describe it as that huge hole and trying to hold on to him is

46

something I think we can all visualize. That had to be very wearing and tearing on you.

LINDSEY: I don't think I realized how emotionally draining it was until years later. But while I was in it, it just felt like life. I was trying to save him, and I wasn't alone in it. He wanted to be saved. I remember when this was going on with Daniel, rehabs weren't around.

RANDY: They weren't readily accessible.

LINDSEY: So, we would take him to the hospital, and it would be a three-day psych hold, and then they would release him. It just felt like there wasn't a lot of help. That show, "Intervention," had come out, and we signed him up to be on it. We never got a call back, but he was the one who came to me and said, "Hey Lindsey, maybe I can get help this way." He really wanted help and there just wasn't a place to turn.

RANDY: I remember how often the seventy-two-hour hold was used—and it is still used today—but I think it was more prevalent then and used more. There was no treatment. It was just a matter of being watched over. There was no real help; it was simply a band-aid, but at least it got him through the next three days.

> "Often, stimulants such as methamphetamines and phencyclidine (PCP) cause violent outbursts in their users. This can cause others to feel in danger. Psychiatric holds can be used to place a loved one struggling with substance abuse in a safe environment that can help them medically detox and come down from an aggressive high."
>
> (Alternative Meds Center. n.d. "Is a Psychiatric Hold Necessary? Common Reasons Someone Could Experience a Psychiatric Hold." Accessed May 4, 2023, https://www.alternativetomeds.com/blog/psychiatric-hold-

LINDSEY: We spent a lot of years back and forth. Daniel never had one drug that he just latched on to. It was whatever was available. So, it was always a roller coaster, up and down, "What's he on now?" It got to the point where I could hear it in his voice if he would call. I would know if he was on uppers or downers just from hearing his voice. It got very tiring trying to save someone. Even though they may want help, it seems like they make it their job as an addict to trick and deceive you. And whether they mean to manipulate you or not, you're being manipulated.

RANDY: You were fighting harder for him than he was fighting for himself.

LINDSEY: Yes. I remember finding out who drug dealers were and I would block the numbers from his phone. I remember answering the phone if he was sleeping, and I would say, "If you sell my husband drugs again, I will call the police on you." I was tracking him down. Following him. You know, looking back on it, who did I think I was? I couldn't save him. My ego was so big to think that.

"According to the 2013 National Survey on Drug Use and Health, around 24.6 million people are in a marriage where one spouse is an addict."

"One of the most challenging situations a couple can face is when the addict isn't ready to change. It's crucial to remember that addiction is a mental illness, not something your partner engages in for trivial or spiteful reasons."

"Although your partner's addiction may feel personal or as if they are discounting your fears and concerns, they struggle internally. Typically, addicts are not ready to face the reality of their situation."

"No one can force an addict to change because they must want to change for themselves. However, there are ways you can help them start the process."

"Educate yourself on addiction and learn about the critical dangers of the substance your partner is using. Provide your partner with resources, even if they initially discard them. Gentle reminders and exposure to sober living can slowly encourage your spouse over time."

Continued...

> "You can also speak with their friends and family about the issue and get them on board. There may come a time when an intervention will be effective, so getting other people in their life involved is essential."
>
> "You can also consult with a professional addiction interventionist to ensure your intervention is as successful as possible."
>
> "The road to treatment for your partner may be messy and even painful, but ultimately it will be worth the effort if your partner decides to work towards a healthy, sober life."
>
> (AddictionHelp.Com. n.d. "Addiction and Divorce." Accessed May 4, 2023, https://www.addictionhelp.com/addiction/divorce)

RANDY: You mentioned something just a moment ago; how he had that voice to where you could tell immediately if it was an upper, a downer, whatever the case may be. Recently, I interviewed someone who was in your seat, and they made a comment about their dad who had been an alcoholic with lots of other drugs involved for years. But she remembers the day after he went to treatment and got clean, he had his *voice* back, as she remembered. I bet you longed for that, didn't you?

LINDSEY: Oh yeah, every day. My parents would see me struggle. One thing my mom said to me that's always stuck with me is, "Honey, I was so worried about you, but you always had a smile on your face. So, I thought everything was OK as long as you were smiling." I probably was good at hiding it from the world.

RANDY: You were in some denial as well. You were probably thinking, "If I don't say it and if I don't show it, maybe it's not real. Or at least I can keep the secret."

LINDSEY: Yes, and it was a secret. After he passed, his stepmom said, "You hid it so well from us. We didn't know what a problem he had." Lilly and I would go to the mall sometimes. And it got to the point where we would drive around waiting for him to fall asleep because it was so embarrassing if he came to the mall with us. He was very vocal when he was on something, and very friendly. And it would get to the point where it was embarrassing. So, we would just leave him in the car, and we would go inside. When Lilly and I would go on a walk or something, we would have to check to make sure he was breathing when we got home. At the time you don't realize how much that is draining you. But it was like a big sigh of relief when we got divorced and I thought, "How did I put my child through this?"

> "The University of Buffalo's Clinical and Research Institute on Addictions discovered that alcohol and substance use are among the most common reasons for divorce—the third-most common reason for women and the eighth-most common for men."
>
> (AddictionHelp.Com. n.d. "Addiction and Divorce." Accessed May 4, 2023, https://www.addictionhelp.com/addiction/divorce)

RANDY: So, go ahead and tell us some about Daniel's last days and how his passing took place.

LINDSEY: Well, there were a lot of good years with Daniel. It might sound like it was all bad, but it wasn't. Daniel had so many good qualities. He was the best boyfriend I ever had, a wonderful provider, and a good father. The addiction just got in the way a lot. At one point, I finally had to divorce Daniel. That was a traumatic time because he fell even farther down the rabbit hole. He became homeless, and he ended up on the news on TV. Then one day, I think maybe he hit rock bottom. I don't know, but he decided to get sober. So, he went to rehab. When he got out, he stayed with his family in Redkey. He stayed sober for a year. He helped me with Jameson. He helped me with Lilly. He was back in Lilly's life. We were best friends again. Things were looking up. He had a job. Then one day Lilly had a school event or something, and we asked him to go out to dinner. Normally, Daniel would have jumped on that because he didn't get to spend a lot of time with Lilly. But he didn't, and I thought, "That's strange. That's not like him." I should have seen that as the first sign of a relapse. A few days later, he showed up at one of Lilly's volleyball games, and I could tell he was not sober. So, I had a long talk with him. I said, "Daniel, I really want to come and get whatever it is you have at home and throw it away and you go to rehab tomorrow." He agreed he would do that, and he did give up what he had—his stash, or whatever—but he didn't go to rehab the next day. It kind of progressed the next couple of weeks when he wouldn't answer the phone. He wouldn't answer text messages. One morning, his stepmom called and said, "Daniel relapsed. He's in the hospital. He's OK, but he did relapse." I just thought, "Oh, here we go again." Then a couple of minutes later, she called back and said, "I'm sorry. I was misinformed. He's no longer with us." It was crushing—just crushing—because I thought we had him back.

"Daniel Rogers

Nov. 28, 1977-Nov. 3, 2018

Paul Daniel Rogers, age 40, of rural Redkey, passed away Saturday morning at IU Health Jay.

He was born in Muncie on Nov. 28, 1977, the son of Jerry Rogers and Ruth McIntire. He worked for FCC (Adams) in Berne and was a journeyman electrician and member of IEBW Electrical Union. He served in the U.S. Marine Corps and was a 1997 Jay County High School graduate.

Surviving are his daughter Lilly Rogers of Redkey; father and step-mother Jerry and Kelly Rogers of Redkey; mother Ruth Paul of Fort Myers, Florida; three brothers, Christopher Rogers (wife: Kaitlyn) of Muncie, James Rogers (wife: Jill) of Keystone and Matthew Rogers (wife: Alicia) of Alcoa, Tennessee; three sisters, Katherine Berkey (husband: Mark) of Fort Wayne, Kristin Seiter (husband: Paul) of Redkey and Angela Rogers of Redkey; cousin David McIntire of Greenwood; and several nieces and nephews."

(TheCR.Com. Tuesday, November 6, 2018. "Daniel Rogers." https://thecr.com/Content/Obituaries/Obituaries/Article/Daniel -Rogers/9/37/64898)

RANDY: So many times, I've heard similar stories where you have those months or that year of recovery, and then there's that relapse that is the *last* relapse, and it takes their lives. I know for a fact that as someone stops using, their resistance to the drug declines dramatically to where using half as much as what they used to use can kill them twice as fast. I think that's the case in many of the overdose deaths. They used to use it so much, so they try that again, but now they can't handle it. Triggers will set them off. We don't always know what sets them off. But going through that, and watching your daughter go through that, had to be traumatic and painful.

LINDSEY: Oh, it was terrible. It was such a battle inside because so many people are judging you. They're watching you. They think they know what's best. And when you love someone so much and you've known them for so many years, it's hard to walk away. So, people try to put themselves in your position, and they think, "Well, I would have just left him." Well, I had Lilly begging me, "Please don't leave Daddy. Please stay." As a human with compassion, how do you leave someone when they're at their absolute worst? It was, "What would God want me to do?" That's a question that came into my mind so many times over the years: "What would God want?" Leaving him when he was so wounded never felt right. But I've never felt so judged in my life, to love him.

RANDY: After Daniel, I know that you had someone else come into your life. Tell us about your relationship with Justin.

LINDSEY: When Daniel and I got divorced, it was literally one of the hardest things I've ever done. So, when this bright light, this ray of hope, Justin, walks in… He was just so happy and charismatic and funny and clever. And he just took my mind off everything that was going on at home. He loved my daughter. My daughter eventually loved him, even though it took a little time. It felt like life was moving forward in a positive way, finally.

RANDY: So, you guys were together for how long?

LINDSEY: Four years

RANDY: I know that you've already made it clear just what a joy he was, and I think a bright light is the way you referred to him. I get that part of it. I knew him well enough to see that in him. He did have that style about him. He was a good "schmoozer." He was fun to be around. He always had a jab for you of some type but was always respectful with it as well. But I know he had his own battles. Tell us a little about that, Lindsey.

LINDSEY: I didn't know Justin growing up. I only knew him from what I saw. He was in the military, and he got hurt in the military. So, the doctor prescribed him pain medication. When Justin and I got together, I knew that he was on medication for his knee. But I didn't think that was an issue because it wasn't drugs from the street. As time went on, I think somehow he had lost his prescription—like his doctor quit writing his prescription or something—and it wasn't long after that that I started noticing a huge change in Justin. He would sleep a lot. He wasn't present. He wouldn't answer my phone calls. He wouldn't show up at Lilly's games, and it was out of character. But we already loved him at that point, and it was, "Not again, God. Not again." But that's where we were.

RANDY: I hear you say, "Not again. Not again." Did you start to doubt or question yourself in any way?

LINDSEY: I did.

RANDY: What was that like for you, Lindsey?

LINDSEY: I just thought, "What is wrong with my choices?" or "What am I supposed to be learning from this?" It was always about Lindsey instead of seeing the bigger picture and seeing that there were two humans struggling so hard that they ended up losing their lives. And I was worried about what people around me thought. You have this idea of what a relationship should feel like, and it should be pretty equal. I think so anyway. The give and take should be even. It just felt like, "I'm always giving and it's not coming back to me." I think I was selfish in that way. I couldn't take myself out of the situation and look at the big picture. And maybe if I could have looked at the big picture, I could have helped.

RANDY: You were a piece of the puzzle instead of being able to stand back and look at the puzzle. You were just too close to it.

LINDSEY: Yes

RANDY: Tell us about Justin's passing.

LINDSEY: I had Jameson. We got pregnant with Jameson about a year before. Justin worked on the road. He was a millwright, so he was gone a lot. He would come home on the weekends. After we had Jameson, he got to take a little time off. It seems like he was switching jobs or companies because he would get to be home more. After we had Jameson, I couldn't work anymore. And I had been kind of used to keeping the finances. I was kind of the breadwinner, I guess. On about day twelve, after Jameson was born, I said, "Justin, honey, you really need to go back to work." He did not want to leave Jameson and Lilly, and me. I think if he could have found a job closer to home, then maybe. But the thought of leaving Jameson when he was just born was hard on him. I started noticing him having a lot more stress, but he went ahead and left. The night that he left, he called, and we had a long talk. We were on the phone until a little after midnight, and then we'd made plans to go see him that weekend. Finally, we hung up the phone. He'd always send me a text message like, "Have a good day at work." And the next morning, I didn't get that text message. I just thought, "Well, it's his first day at a new job." At lunchtime, he would always call, and that day I didn't get a phone call at lunch. But I kept telling myself, "Everything's OK." Then, I got a phone call from Dan Watson.

RANDY: This is Justin's dad?

LINDSEY: Yes. And he said, "Lindsey, I'm going to need you to come to the house." I said, "No. I'm not coming over, Dan." I knew something was wrong. He called back and said, "Lindsey, I need you to come to the house." I finally went to the house and found out Justin had passed.

RANDY: We understand that was an overdose. We don't know what triggered it, and so many times we don't. What did it trigger in you when you knew that he was gone?

LINDSEY: I had our newborn baby, Jameson, and Lilly. I was heartbroken and devastated. I did not see it. Justin had such a huge problem. I did not see it or didn't want to see it. With Daniel, I always kind of knew, in the back of my mind, "At some point, he's probably not going to make it." I had come to grips with that. With Justin, it blindsided me.

RANDY: He'd been doing well before that, for a while, hadn't he?

LINDSEY: I think so. Justin was very secretive. He was very good at that. But I really think he had been doing better. I knew I had to be strong for the baby and for Lilly. Lilly had already been through a lot in her life, and then to lose Justin; I knew it was going to be traumatic. I just knew that I needed to be strong for them.

RANDY: Those two hits… I can't imagine how hard they were to take; to lose one child's father to a drug overdose, and then to lose your other child's father to a drug overdose. The toughness is beyond my ability to imagine. Who did you become after all of that?

LINDSEY: Numb. Very numb. I kind of locked myself away for four years. I just focused on the kids and dealing with myself. I would look at myself in the mirror and think, "Why is my life here? What could I have done differently? What could I have changed? What was my part in it?" It took a long time to reflect on that, and it's hard to look at yourself in the mirror.

RANDY: Yes. That's one of the most difficult moments anyone can have, and to enjoy what you see. So, you mentioned how you'd kind of locked yourself away for those four years; a lot of introspection, trying to figure out whatever you could figure out with this. Where are you today? Who are you now? What's your mental state? What's your emotional state? I know there's still pain. You'll never get over the loss of either one of them. You loved them too much to get over it. But where are you now?

LINDSEY: I think I'm in a good spot. Jameson is in preschool now, and his grandmother, Kelly, watches him so that I can work. I got to go back to work, and I think that was a huge step in my mental wellness. I've realized that I was not in control of any of it. The way that I reacted, which was with a lot of anger most of the time. I fought a lot with Daniel and Justin, which is what I was capable of at that time.

RANDY: It was the best you could do under your circumstances, knowing what you knew.

LINDSEY: Yes. I think that every day, whatever you feel guilty about or whatever you're struggling with, you have to think, "Did I do my best? Was my intention the best?" And I see that I only did what I was capable of at the time. So, I've made peace with that.

RANDY: That's had to be a journey, in and of itself, and I'm going to guess—though you're at the point of peace—that journey's going to continue with every breath you have. Hopefully, it will grow and improve, and you will understand yourself better than you ever have; that you will be the you that God created you to be, and you will no longer feel anger at them or yourself. We make mistakes. That's called life, but it's what we do with those mistakes, yes?

LINDSEY: Yes. It's amazing, the steps that you go through when you lose someone. What are those called?

RANDY: The stages of grief.

The Stages of Grief:
- "Denial - For some people, this may be the first response to loss. As an immediate reaction, you might doubt the reality of the loss at first. After this first reaction of shock and denial, you may go numb for a while. At some point, you could feel like nothing matters to you anymore. Life as you once knew it has changed. It might be difficult to feel you can move on. The first stage of grief is a natural reaction that helps you process the loss in your own time. By going numb, you're giving yourself time to explore at your own pace the changes you're going through. Denial is a temporary response that carries you through the first wave of pain. Eventually, when you're ready, the feelings and emotions you have denied will resurface, and your healing journey will continue."
- "Anger - Feeling intensely angry might surprise you or your loved ones, but it's not uncommon. This anger serves a purpose. It might be particularly overwhelming for some people to feel anger because, in many cultures, anger is a feared or rejected emotion. You might be more used to avoiding it than confronting it. During the anger stage of grief, you might start asking questions like "Why me?" or "What did I do to deserve this?" You could also feel suddenly angry at inanimate objects, strangers, friends, or family members. You might feel angry at life itself. It's not rare to also feel anger toward the situation or person you lost.

Continued...

Rationally, you might understand the person isn't to blame. Emotionally, however, you may resent them for causing you pain or for leaving you. At some point, you might also feel guilty for being angry. This could make you angrier."

- "Bargaining - Bargaining is a stage of grief that helps you hold on to hope in a situation of intense pain. You might think to yourself that you're willing to do anything and sacrifice everything if your life is restored to how it was before the loss. During this internal negotiation, you could find yourself thinking in terms of "what if" or "if only": what if I did XYZ, then everything will go back to normal; if only I had done something differently to prevent the loss. Guilt might be an accompanying emotion during this stage as you inadvertently might be trying to regain some control, even if at your own expense."

- "Depression - In this instance, depression isn't a sign of a mental health condition. Instead, it's a natural and appropriate response to grief. During the depression stage, you start facing your present reality and the inevitability of the loss you've experienced. Understandably, this realization may lead you to feel intense sadness and despair. This intense sadness could cause you to feel different in other aspects too.
  - o You could feel:
    - fatigued
    - vulnerable
    - confused and distracted
    - not wanting to move on
    - not hungry or wanting to eat
    - not able or willing to get ready in the morning
    - not able to enjoy what you once did"

Continued…

- "Acceptance - Reaching acceptance isn't necessarily about being OK with what happened. Depending on your experience, it might be understandable if you don't ever feel this way. Acceptance is more about how you acknowledge the losses you've experienced, how you learn to live with them, and how you readjust your life accordingly. You might feel more comfortable reaching out to friends and family during this stage, but it's also natural to feel you prefer to withdraw at times. You may also feel like you accept the loss at times and then move to another stage of grief again. This back-and-forth between stages is natural and a part of the healing process. In time, you may eventually find yourself stationed at this stage for long periods of time. That doesn't mean you'll never feel sadness or anger again toward your loss, but your long-term perspective about it and how you live with this reality will be different."

(PsychCentral. n.d. "Mourning the 5 Stages of Grief." Accessed May 4, 2023, https://psychcentral.com/lib/the-5-stages-of-loss-and-grief#Going-through-the-5-stages-of-grief:-How-it-feels)

LINDSEY: Yes. They are true. You go through every single one of those, and sometimes you revisit them.

RANDY: It's not always a linear movement. You bounce back and forth.

LINDSEY: There are still times I think I might be in denial, thinking, "Maybe Justin will come back"—not as Justin, but as, like, this new soul. And, then I think, "Lindsey! What?" It's just denial.

RANDY: Yes, that is part of it. That is denial, but it's also coping. And it's not the worst of ways to cope with this. So many don't have any tools to cope with it, and at least you're thinking about the grief by mentioning those stages; that denial, that anger, and when you get to the end, reinvesting in life. Lindsey, I recognize that your being here today cannot be an easy thing. It can't be comfortable, but you're wanting to invest in life. You started this whole thing off today with the idea that you want to help kids whose parents are struggling with addiction. Do you have any further thoughts on that and how you might be able to play that out?

LINDSEY: For a long time, I thought, "Well, Lilly had some friends that were in the same situation, and maybe if we just had a little group every week where they met." It never really went much further than just her friends, but I've often thought about that. I've also looked into getting my master's in social work because that's the quickest way I could get to counseling. I'm not sure that's where I'm intended to go.

RANDY: Lindsey, thank you for your willingness to join us and share, and open up. This is so appreciated. And I know it's going to have an impact because there are many folks out there like you, who fought the battle for someone or with someone but didn't come out with the victory they'd hoped for. Once again, we appreciate it. God bless you.

Chapter 4

Lilly Rogers– "I just wanted a dad."

"Likewise, you who are younger, be subject to the elders. Clothe yourselves, all of you, with humility toward one another, for "God opposes the proud but gives grace to the humble."
(1 Pet. 5:5 NIV)

Within eighteen months, middle-schooler, Lilly Rogers, lost two very important men in her life to drug overdoses. First was Justin Watson, her mother's boyfriend, and the father of her half-brother. Justin was found dead in his hotel room. Lilly called Justin "Second Dad." A few months later, Daniel Rogers, her biological father also overdosed. Against all odds, Lilly has come through the back-to-back tragedies healthy and strong. This is her story.

RANDY: Today, we have a young lady with us by the name of Lilly Rogers. She's at a good place in her life, but to get to that good place, she's gone through a lot of struggles, hurt, and loss. To have her with us should say a lot to anybody and everybody who is out there struggling. So, Lilly, welcome today.

LILLY: Thank you, Randy.

RANDY: Our pleasure to have you with us. Why don't you go ahead and introduce yourself. Just share a bit about who you are, your age, where you go to school, and what you do at school.

LILLY: I go to Jay County High School. I'm a junior. I'm sixteen years old, and I'm in cheer. I live with my mom and my little brother.

RANDY: I know cheerleading has been a big part of your life. Tell us about that.

LILLY: I've been in cheer since fifth grade, and I love it so much. It's like an escape from what's going on in my life. I can go there, and I can talk to all my friends and be with the coaches. Just having the team has helped a lot.

RANDY: That's a safe place, yes? A place where you find that peace and that comfort the rest of the world's not giving you?

LILLY: Yes.

RANDY: Neat. Listen, I know this is going to be tough for you, and it's going to be tough for the folks who are listening. Let's go back several years. Tell us about yourself as a young child. You said you started with cheer in fifth grade but tell us more about you at that age.

LILLY: My family lived in this big, white, house on the highway, and when I was about four years old, we moved to the house we live in now. I would say that was when our family really came together. It was Mom and Dad and me. We had those few good years, where we were just a family. We had our new house, and it was just good.

RANDY: That was a comfortable time for you. I remember your dad well. I coached your dad, and he was a classmate of one of my boys. And, of course, being there in the community, I always had respect for him. I felt the same respect in return. But I know that he got into some issues, some addictions, and struggles. Tell us about that. Tell us how it affected you, and how it affected family life; the hurts, the pains, the fears. Just go ahead and open up, because I know there are young people out there that you'll be able to relate to that none of the rest of us can.

LILLY: Well, when his addiction started, I was young. I didn't really know what addiction was. I just knew that when I would come home from school or anything, I would want to make sure that my dad was OK. I knew that there was something wrong, but I didn't know how bad or exactly what was wrong.

RANDY: So, did you just see it as some sort of sickness, and you wanted to check to make sure he was OK?

LILLY: When I was young, I thought he took medicine, and that the medicine was to make him feel better and make him act right. I didn't realize that it was his addiction, or that it was a bad thing. I just thought, "You know, it's normal. He's taking his medicine." Once I started getting older, I started realizing, "You know, this isn't right. This isn't how this should go." Sometimes I would be at home when Mom was at work, and he would be sitting there talking to me, watching SpongeBob with me, making me toast, and then suddenly, he would just fall asleep. I wouldn't know what to do. He was just sitting there and then he'd start falling asleep, and it was scary. So, I would call Mom or Grandma or Grandpa, and someone would come down and check on me and take me with them. But sitting there as a little kid, not knowing what was wrong with him and not knowing if he was going to be OK affected me a lot. Sometimes friends couldn't come over because he wasn't in the right mind to be around people.

RANDY: How old were you then?

LILLY: Maybe six or seven.

RANDY: Did you start to recognize any feelings that you didn't know what to do with, or were you still just accepting all of that as health needs, as far as the pills?

LILLY: I think it kind of started once I was getting to that age. I started realizing Mom and Dad would fight a lot, and other than the addiction, there wasn't much to fight about. They were good people, and they were good together. But with his addiction, it just kind of pulled them apart. She loved him, and you could tell he loved her. But when the addiction was around, he just wasn't himself.

RANDY: Makes total sense, and I can almost picture that. Let's move on a little bit in your life as you begin to realize and recognize, "This is more than a healthcare need, as far as this medicine is going."

LILLY: I knew Dad was a good person and I knew that he loved me. I knew that he wanted to be there for us, but as I started getting older the anger came. When I was young, I thought, "Oh, it's just my dad. He's here for us. He loves us." But then I started realizing, "This is not good," and I got angry. I could not understand why he couldn't just stop. I couldn't understand why, if he loved us enough, he didn't just stop. I thought, "If he wants to be in our family and be there for us, then he can just stop doing

63

it." To me, it was a choice, like "that or us." But then I started to realize that it wasn't that easy. He couldn't just pick us over drugs because it was, in a way, a sickness.

> "In the United States, about one in eight children, ages seventeen or younger are living in households with at least one parent who has a substance use disorder."
>
> (National Center on Substance Abuse and Child Welfare. n.d. "Children and Families Affected by Parental Substance Use Disorders (SUDs)." Accessed May 4, 2023, https://ncsacw.acf.hhs.gov/topics/parental-substance-use-disorder.aspx)

RANDY: Did you, at any time, have a confrontation with him, saying something like, "Hey, you can stop this. You're going to have to choose between it and us."

LILLY: I did. It was probably around the time that Mom and Dad got a divorce. At that time, I was eight. He told me—he sat me down—and he said, "Me and your mom are going to get a divorce." And I was upset, and I just told him that I didn't understand why he couldn't stop, why there were so many problems, and he couldn't fix them. Once the divorce was final, and he wasn't really there anymore, there were multiple times that he got arrested on drug-related charges. I would call him, and I would be so mad at him. I'd tell him, I'd say, "Dad, why can't you just choose us? We miss you. We want you to be OK. Just choose us."

RANDY: So, as you tried your best to deal with that and to recognize and realize, "Dad does have a real problem of some type." Did you start to come to recognize that as a disease?

LILLY: Yes. Especially because I thought all this time that it was just a problem, and it could get fixed. As I've gotten older, I can now see that it wasn't just something that he could fix easily. He went to rehab. He went to Brianna's Hope. He did try. But every single time it was like the addiction won. It started to make sense to me that it wasn't just something he could fix. It was something that he had to fight against, and it was more like a disease than just a problem.

RANDY: That's insightful for someone at your age. Of course, now, as you look back, your vision is more twenty-twenty than it was then. You didn't know what you didn't know at that age. And it's your dad, somebody you believe in, someone you trust, someone who is trying to lead, guide, and direct you. And he can't even do that in his own life because of it. I can't imagine what the frustration must have been. What was your outlet during that time? How did you vent your pain? How did you deal with your hurt?

LILLY: My grandma and grandpa. When Dad wasn't doing well, Mom had to pick up another job. She worked at the Commercial Review Newspaper, and then she started working at this little restaurant. During that time, I couldn't stay with Dad, so I would stay with Grandma and Grandpa. I was there from as soon as I got out of school until eight or nine o'clock at night. They were there for me to talk to, and they understood. I knew I could always talk to them.

RANDY: They played the role that grandparents can play. They can separate themselves, even amidst the hurt. I'm convinced that a grandparent's happiness is based on the happiness of their grandkids, and they certainly proved it throughout that situation. So, as time progressed, I know that your dad continued to fight that battle, to deal with his addiction. Take us to the next step.

LILLY: I was in middle school, and he was still in and out of his drug problems and his drug use. It was eighth grade, and he had sobered up. He had been sober for about a year. I was mad at him because of all the years that he wasn't there and all the years that he wasn't sober. I probably wasn't the nicest to him. You know, I said some things that I didn't mean. I didn't really want to be around him all that much because I was scared that I was going to get hurt again and that he was going to go back. Really, towards the beginning, I didn't want to be around him unless Mom was there. I didn't want to get too close. Once he hit a year of being sober, we had this party for him and this cake and it kind of hit me, "Maybe he's going to be OK. He's made it to a year. This is the

65

longest he's ever been sober." I felt like I got to know the real him without the addiction, and I let myself get close to him. Our family had a wedding, and we went to that together. We danced and had fun. I was just so happy that I had that moment with him that I forgot about all the hurt and the sadness. At that time, I got to make some good memories of him being him.

RANDY: How precious. You know, all those pent-up feelings… it sounds like you kind of let go of them on the dance floor.

LILLY: Yeah, and he was always so goofy when I was little, and just always dancing and singing and just having a good time. I kind of missed it. When they got divorced, and he moved out on his own, I didn't get to see that for a while. And when he sobered back up, it just showed how really goofy and fun he could be.

RANDY: Everything inside him came out in a good way during that time. OK, you said he was like a year clean, there. You had the wedding, and that was such a wonderful time and a precious memory. Take us to your dad's passing.

LILLY: I was in cheer, and it was my eighth-grade year, so I had Eighth Grade Night. Your parents would walk you out and you would get gifts and it was pretty much like, "Hey, you completed eighth grade! We're proud of you!" At this point, Dad was doing good, so I asked him to come and walk me out with Mom. He showed up late. When he showed up, you could just tell, you know, he had relapsed. He was messed up. He wasn't himself. I was so angry at him—so angry. Mom told him he couldn't walk me out like that in front of all these people. She told him he needed to go home, and he needed to get himself together. After it was over, I called him. I was just so mad at him, and I was yelling and screaming. And I said, "I can't do this anymore! I can't let you be a part of my life if you're going to continually walk out of it every couple of years or every couple of months!" It was emotionally draining, and I just couldn't do it anymore. I told him that. A couple of weeks later I started to feel bad. I was like, "I can't believe I said those things to him. I didn't mean it. I want to take it back." So, I texted him and said, "Dad, I love you and I want you to be OK. I just don't want to get hurt again. I want us to be like how we were this whole year." He texted me back, and he said that he had moved in with his girlfriend who he had met at his job, but that he wanted me to come to meet her. He acted like he was doing well, but I thought by the text message he sent me back that he was not doing well. So, the night I texted him, I was staying the night with my friend. My friend and my mom and I were all going to get breakfast the next morning. So, I woke up and called my mom. I'm like, "Hey Mom, are we going to go get breakfast?" She was like, "Yeah, I need to talk to your friend's mom." I was like, "OK, I'll go tell her and I'll have her call you." So, I go down there, and I told her that my mom needed to talk to her. Once she got off the phone with my mom, she came and took my phone. She said, "I can't have you on your phone right now. I need it. Your mom is going to be here soon." So, my friend and I were like, "What's going on? We had these plans." So, I went to get ready, and I walked downstairs, and in walked my mom and I just looked at her and I knew something was wrong. I was scared that it was my grandpa because he had just gotten out of the hospital for medical problems, and I said, "Is it Dad or is it Grandpa?" She just said, "It's your dad." And I just fell apart. My whole world just came crumbling down. It was shattered. I knew without her saying that he had passed away, that he was gone. It was like I could just feel that that part of me wasn't there anymore if that makes sense.

RANDY: It makes total sense. Just a sudden emptiness, does that describe it?

LILLY: Yes.

RANDY: I know there are a lot of feelings that follow that, that you had to go through. This was an overdose death, yes?

LILLY: Yes

RANDY: You had to go through some feelings of anger. "Why did you do this to yourself? Why did you do it to me?"

LILLY: Yeah. At first, I was so hurt. I didn't even know how to deal with it. I was like, "This is just so much. He was here for so long, and even if they weren't the best years, he's gone now." I had to think about how I'm never going to get that hug that he gives. He gave the most amazing hugs; just hugged you so hard.

Then, after the hurt, I was angry. I was like, "Why couldn't he just stay sober?" He had made it to a year, and he was doing good, and we had those good times, and now it was all gone. And there was nothing he could do to even fix it because he was gone.

RANDY: You had to be feeling a sense of loss. During that, what brought you out of those darkest moments? What was your healing, your help?

LILLY: It was hard there for like a year. I was sad. I'd go from angry to sad, crying to Mom and then getting mad. I think just having my family, you know, with Mom and Grandma and Grandpa. And, I had my little brother. And he just brought so much sunshine to everything. He was only a year old at the time, and he didn't know anything except being happy. He was just always laughing and playing.

RANDY: That's neat; that innocence. And the way it was able to lift you up and help you maintain some sort of strength, help, and promise for the future. Was that the first person close to you that had passed away, Lilly?

LILLY: No, it wasn't.

RANDY: What was the relationship with the other person that passed?

LILLY: He was like my stepdad. It was my mom's boyfriend. He came around about the time my mom and dad got divorced. He came around and kind of just stepped up when my dad was out. His name was Justin, and I think the thing I remember most about him is his beard. I know that's weird, but he had this red beard. And it just kind of made him who he was. It was the thing that stood out. The first time I ever met him, he came to the house, and I was crying because I wanted McDonald's. I was hungry and Mom wasn't taking me to McDonald's, and I was mad.

RANDY: Shame on Mom!

LILLY: I know! He got there and he saw me crying about McDonald's, so he took me to McDonald's. He had this black Malibu, and I thought his car was so cool. It had tinted windows and everything. And I got in there and we were listening to music, and he took me to get McDonald's.

RANDY: Was it just the two of you?

LILLY: Oh, no. Mom was there too. When we got back to the house, we wanted to watch a movie. We made this big pallet on the floor with blankets and pillows, and we all laid there and watched a movie, and then I fell asleep.

RANDY: What role did Justin play in your life and with your mom?

LILLY: He was in the Army, and he had this huge bag. I liked Justin, but I wasn't comfortable with him just moving in, just coming. I didn't want Mom to move on from Dad because I felt like it was us just letting Dad go. And I did not like that. So, Justin would walk in with this huge Army bag, and I'd get so mad because it would have all his clothes in it for like the whole entire week. And I'd be like, "Why is he here? I don't want him here! He needs to take that Army bag and leave!" I just knew that when he had the Army bag, he was staying for a while, and I didn't like it. He'd discipline me. Dad wasn't there enough to discipline me. But Justin made me do the dishes, pick up my clothes, and help Mom.

RANDY: He was horrible, wasn't he?

LILLY: I know! At the time, I thought, "This is terrible!" Two years in of me not liking him and him making me do chores and making me respect Mom, and then I started to like him. I was like, "Well, this is different. I think he's OK." He would play with me and my friends. We would play tag or hide-and-go-seek outside, and he would help me hide. He would build us campfires and build us a tent outside, so we could stay outside for the night. He was just becoming a good guy, and I was like, "This is good." But then he started doing drugs as well. The first time, it was either his birthday or Christmas. I'm not sure. I cannot remember which one. Mom and I were driving through town and saw him pulled over. He was outside of the car, and he had on handcuffs. He was getting arrested. It was just the same thing all over again. We had to deal with this again; the addiction, the getting hurt. By this time, I already loved him. It was too late to be like, "Oh, I still don't like him." He had stepped in. He was "Dad" when Dad couldn't be there. I called him "Second Dad," and I was invested at this point. And it was just so much seeing that.

RANDY: That had to set off a lot of triggers. It had to bring up a lot of memories that you had tried to suppress and somewhat forget. And it had to make you think, "Here we are again." Let's go on from that moment of him being arrested.

LILLY: I think if it wasn't Christmas, then he did get arrested on Christmas again. So, we were around him for four years and we only got one Christmas with him. Because somehow, every Christmas, he was either in jail or messed up with his drug use. It was just hard because he started not being there like how Dad started not being there. All this time, I was so mad at Dad. And I was so happy that Justin was there, and then Justin wasn't there. And I was so mad at both of them. It was like, "Why can't I just have the dad figure be there and not mess it up?" You know, my whole life, I just wanted a dad who was there, like my friends had. The dad who went out and played basketball with you, and I thought that was Justin. And he just… yeah….

RANDY: The dream and the hope had been broken. With the closeness you started to have with him, you started to gain trust in him. And suddenly it is torn apart and ripped out from under you. Is that accurate?

LILLY: Yes. So, he went to Brianna's Hope, and he was trying to get it together. I think it was a year that his addiction was bad, and he tried getting it back together. Justin and I wanted Mom to have a baby. So, we convinced her. We said, "Mom, we want a little kid. We want a baby around." And, she was not having it. She said, "I don't want a baby. I don't want to go through this." By this time, I was about twelve. And she would say, "You're almost all grown up and I'd have to start all over again." So, you know, it took a lot of convincing. We just kept saying, "Mom, we want a baby. Come on! Have a kid!" And eventually, she did. She got pregnant. I remember it was Thanksgiving. We were on our way to my aunt's house, and I said, "Mom, I think you're pregnant." And she goes, "No I'm not, Lilly." So, I said, "Then stop and get a pregnancy test and prove to me that you're not pregnant." She did, and she was pregnant! It just changed everything. There was going to be another human living in our house. Justin was going to be a dad to his biological son. And it felt like, "Maybe Justin is going to be OK. He's going to see that Mom's having a son, and he's going to just step up." And, for a little bit, he did. He started fixing things around the house. He started putting the room together for Jameson, and he just really stepped up. He was really getting it together. He worked on the road, so he was kind of in and out, going to different places. There was this one night that he had left. He was on the road, so he had to make sure that everything was done before he left. He made sure that the new lights were hanging up and that Jameson's room was put together. He wanted everything to be OK before he left. He left, and that night I walked into Mom's room. It was like midnight, and she was sitting there on her bed, giggling on the phone. I said, "Who are you on the phone with?" She said, "I'm on the phone with Justin." I said, "Oh my gosh, you guys are like a bunch of teenagers." I was laughing at them. He wanted us to—I think he was in Cincinnati. He was in Ohio somewhere—and he wanted us to come there. He wanted to take Jameson to the zoo. He wanted us to just come up there for the weekend, and we said it was the plan. We were going to go there. It was Friday, and it was the day that we had the solar eclipse. I was in school, and at that time I played volleyball. Mom came to volleyball practice, and she said, "We need to go." So, we got to the car, and I said, "Mom, what's wrong?" And she just started crying. She couldn't even say what she needed to get out. And I said, "Is something wrong with Jess?" She is Justin's sister. Because I thought there was something wrong with Jess, and she said, "No." I asked her friend that was in the car with her, "What is wrong?" And Mom goes, "Sis, it's just Justin. Justin's gone." And I said, "Like, he's gone to jail? Gone to rehab?" And she said, "No sis, he's just gone." And it hit me, "Oh, Justin's gone. Gone. He's not here anymore." We drove to his parents' house. His mom, Kelly, came running out and just hugged me. It was something that no one expected. We thought he was doing good. He just had Jameson. He was getting everything together, and no one thought that he was going to overdose and die.

RANDY: Sure. The shock of the way things came about. They thought things were better. We never know, obviously, and we never know when that next use is our last use. And for you to endure two losses of such magnitude of people so close—of people important to you, of people you've already said you loved—for you to go through that. What's sustaining you today, Lilly? How do you have the smile you have, the countenance you have? You should be miserable. How are you beating that?

LILLY: I try to think, "I did have those years with them." I had that year with Dad, and I had those years with Justin. And I just try to think, you know, "At least I had those years." I've learned that people don't stay in your life forever. They come and they're here, and then they're gone. I think just realizing that has helped a lot. I go to counseling. Counseling has helped me tremendously. One of my favorite parts of my week is getting to go and talk to my counselor. Jameson just keeps everything so fun. Even when he's throwing a tantrum, I just sit there and laugh at him because he looks ridiculous. He just brings so much light and so much joy to the family. I can't imagine if Jameson wasn't here. If it would have been just me and Mom, I think we would have just crashed and burned. But because of Jameson, we had to stay strong and keep it together and be there for him, and that has helped a lot.

RANDY: What would you like to say to young people out there who may be going through what you have been through or dealing with a parent or parents who are into addiction, and they're trying their best to be there with them, for Mom and Dad. What would you like to say to them?

LILLY: It's hard. It's really hard. Being a kid and going through that is the toughest thing. But, at the end of the day, it makes you stronger. It makes you more mature. I guess I just want kids to know that they can find people to talk to. I'm always open to talk to anybody who has been through this, because of what I've been through. And I never want them to feel like they're alone. There are kids out there that go through this, and they probably don't have anyone to talk to. I would say the best thing is to find someone to talk to, whether it's your grandma, a friend, or an aunt or uncle.

RANDY: Or a counselor…

LILLY: Yes. Even one of us. Mom and I, you know, we're always here for anybody. And I never want them to feel like they're

72

alone. That's one of the worst things, is to feel like there's no one to help.

RANDY: Before our interview started, you were talking about your cheerleading, and we talked about the role that played in your life. But you said as you girls gather at the end of the day, you have—what did you say that was called? That moment where you share yourselves and let go of those struggles?

LILLY: Yeah. We have Circle Time.

RANDY: Yes. Explain Circle Time, because we all need it, whether we're cheerleaders or not.

LILLY: "Circle of Emotions" is what one girl calls it. Right before practice, we all get in a circle, and we take turns and say what was the worst part of our day or just something we need to get off our chests. In that circle, you know that what you're saying isn't going to go anywhere. You can tell them anything and they're going to have your back. Just being a part of that is incredible. I would encourage anyone to be on some sort of team because it's a distraction to take everything away and just focus on that sport. And having a team, it's like, "These girls aren't just my teammates. They're my best friends." Some of them are like my sisters, and just having them be there and being able to talk to them is just amazing.

RANDY: Lilly, you said you're sixteen, right?

LILLY: Yeah

RANDY: Whether you are sixteen, twenty-six, fifty-six, or seventy-six, we need those kinds of moments. We need those kinds of people. We need that kind of community. A big part of any recovery is communication and the idea of being able to share openly and honestly. You may not be in recovery from addiction, but you're certainly in recovery from PTSD from the losses you've suffered. And you're going about it with intent and purpose with the counseling and with having that ring of friends around you, and what you've shared here today. This truly humbles me. I don't mind saying that. To think of a young person going through that. I loved your dad. You know I coached him in peewee football and junior high football. He was part of the community. And as I said, a classmate of our son. And Justin, I coached him, too. I knew him well, and I loved Justin. We had a good relationship. A loss has a ripple effect that we never know about, and so will the words that you've shared here today. There are young people out there that can't even begin to fathom how to deal with what you went through. Your willingness to be vulnerable, to be raw, to be real. That's maturity beyond sixteen, young lady.

LILLY: Thank you

RANDY: Is there anything you'd like to wrap up with? Words of encouragement or just thanksgiving to someone or even final words to Daniel or Justin?

LILLY: Like, what I would want to say to them?

RANDY: Yes

LILLY: I think I would want to tell them that I'm proud of them for fighting for so long and for trying to beat it. I wish I could just tell them one last time that I love them. They've made such an impact on my life that I can never forget them. Those were two of my best friends, two of the most important people in my life. I will forever be thankful for them and how they impacted my life. Even if there were bad things, they taught me lessons. Maybe I was too young then to learn those lessons, but it's helped me a lot today.

RANDY: So, you're not going to focus or identify them by the way they passed. You're going to focus and identify them by the way they loved and the way they shared with you.

LILLY: Yes. The addiction was not who they were. I would never want someone to be like, "Oh yeah, Daniel Rogers, he died from addiction. Justin Watson, the addiction was who he was," because that's not it at all. They had a problem. They had a disease, but it didn't define them. What defined them was their personalities and how they cared and how they loved and how you could always trust them. It is sad that they had a problem, but that's not who they were.

RANDY: Lilly, thank you. Thank you for everything you've shared.

LILLY: Thank you for having me.

RANDY: And folks, we will all be identified in some way, someday. Focus. Focus on the real. Focus on the good. I know it's a struggle. There are days that we just don't even want to get out of bed, or things we don't want to face. But so far, every person that's listening to the sound of my voice or reading this is 100% successful in making it through those days you never thought you'd make it through. If a sixteen-year-old can do it when she went through it at twelve, and then again at fourteen, guess what; you can too. Stay in the battle!

According to Futures Recovery Healthcare, "children can receive help through:
- Alateen, a 12-Step program designed for children with a parent who has SUD or AUD, providing them peer support, coping skills, and encouragement
- Professional therapist, specializing in children (and family addiction)
- Family therapy
- School guidance counselor
- Coach
- Trusted teacher
- Religious leader or member"

"In addition to providing outside support and structure for children with a parent that has a SUD or AUD, there are other steps you can take to help, including:
- Reminding a child that they are loved unconditionally.
- Respecting that even if their parent is in active addiction, children still often love and care for their mom or dad—and that's okay.
- Refraining from saying negative and condemning things about the child's parent (for the reason above).
- Encouraging a child to be a child—providing opportunities for play, recreation, entertainment, and fun activities.

Continued…

- Listening and asking questions, rather than trying to "speak at" a child about his/her parent and situation (Ex: "How does that make you feel?).
- Extending healthy opportunities and resources to express emotion—journaling, walking, running, smashing playdough or clay, stress toys, art, etc."

(Futures Recovery Healthcare. n.d. "Children Living in Families with Addiction Issues." accessed April 3, 2023, https://futuresrecoveryhealthcare.com/blog/children-living-in-families-with-addiction-issues)

Chapter 5

RJ Pitman– "I never really got to be a kid."

"A man without self-control is like a city broken into and left without walls."
(Proverbs 25:28 NIV)

At the age of twelve, RJ started smoking marijuana. By age fourteen, he was using cocaine. At sixteen, he dropped out of school and spent his eighteenth birthday in jail. He then got into dealing drugs and spent several years in prison. By the age of thirty, more than half of his life had been consumed by addiction and the struggles that go with it. Between a supportive probation officer, a strong court team, and a renewed faith in God, RJ was able to find his way into recovery. The battle continues, but as RJ will tell you, "God's got this."

RANDY: Welcome, RJ.

RJ: Thank you for having me.

RANDY: We're anxious to hear what you have to share with us. I know you've been there, done that, and have the scars to prove it. You're living above it now, but I know you had to live with it for a while.

RJ: Absolutely. Addiction is always different for everybody, so I'm sure I'll have something new to share.

RANDY: That's the neat thing about this. We want to be about all things recovery. We know we have to take a sort of throwing the rice approach instead of throwing the rock, and you're a piece of the rice today, in a very good way. Could you tell us about who you are today, and what you're about?

RJ: Today I own a business. It is called Recovery Painting and Remodeling. Note the word recovery. I try to work closely with our court systems and am trying to hire people that need a second chance at getting employment—people that are either in active addiction trying to find recovery or in recovery trying to stay out of active addiction. I also have a non-profit that isn't registered yet with the state, but we're getting there. It's a slow process, as you know. We help people that are in recovery stay there. We throw events. You've been down to those before. We have people come in from all around the country and give testimonials, play music, and stuff like that.

RANDY: Some big name speakers that are very much recognized in the recovery field.

RJ: Yes. We've had Joe Nester. He's huge in the recovery community. Joe has played for us now two years in a row and will be back with us for a third year this fall. Chas Smith, who performs under the name Colicchie—which I think everybody out there in the recovery world knows—we've had him both years as well. Then, of course, B-RAIN, Rim One, and some of our speakers are Chicago Hope Dealers. They came in this year and helped. Minnesota Hope Dealers were there this year.

RANDY: From dope dealers to hope dealers.

RJ: Yes! So now instead of slinging dope, we're slinging hope, right?

RANDY: And that's why we're here today because we believe your story is going to give people hope. We believe that at the very least, more than one struggler is going to be able to identify, and more than one is going to be able to understand something when we're done that they didn't understand before.

RJ: Absolutely. And that's what it's about, touching one person.

RANDY: That'll be the victory. Let's go back to your early days. Let's talk about you as a young person. Tell us what you were about. What was it that fired you up for life during that time?

RJ: Addiction comes in many walks of life. Mine was a little different than what some of the people prior to me went through. I grew up in a decent household. My dad and my mom split up at a young age, but my stepdad stepped up. He played that dad role for many years, so I had a good childhood. Well, all the way until I was about twelve years old when I started self-destructing. That wasn't because of any parenting, but

78

unfortunately, I didn't have that father figure there. I do now, which is great. And my dad's sober now. The walk of life I had in the beginning and then the walk of life we're going to talk about in my active addiction is a complete one-eighty. It just goes to show that anybody can end up battling and winning against this disease, praise God! And it won't be easy, but anybody can get out of that disease.

RANDY: That's why we're here, hashtag addicts do recover. I think I caught you saying that the demise and struggle started at about twelve years of age. Share that with us.

RJ: I was very active in sports when I grew up. I liked to play football, baseball, basketball, any sport. And it didn't matter if they had overlapping seasons. I played them. Luckily, I had my mom and my stepdad that backed that up and put in probably twelve extra hours a day on top of their twelve hours of work to be there. That required me to have the energy to do that. I started off by smoking marijuana. I think a lot of people can relate to that.

RANDY: This is in your junior high years?

RJ: Yes. This is when I was twelve. Very quickly, though, it turned into cocaine use. And that was so I could remain active and keep going.

RANDY: How old were you when it changed to cocaine?

RJ: Fourteen.

RANDY: How were you able to get cocaine? How did you find it? Why the switch from marijuana to cocaine?

RJ: A lot of the people I hung out with had access to cocaine at that time. Back then, we didn't have the random drug screens at the schools like they have now. It was very easy to skid by and not have to worry about getting caught doing any of these things. That's what I did. I got active into cocaine when I was fourteen, and that helped me keep going with lifting weights and doing the things I needed to do to stay active in sports. Unfortunately, that changed because of that active addiction. My thought process was, "I'll just do this until I get through school, and then I'll be done with it." Well, as an addict, with the disease that I carry, that's not feasible, as we all know.

> "Under the Fourth Amendment, the legal website Lawyers.com notes, "public schools generally aren't allowed to search students or their belongings unless they have a 'reasonable suspicion' that the students have broken the law or school rules, and that the search will turn up evidence of that wrongdoing."
>
> "But student-athletes are a special case, which the Supreme Court cited in its ruling in Vernonia (Oregon) School District v. Acton, a 1995 case that upheld the constitutionality of random testing of athletes."
>
> (Ohio University. n.d. "High School Athletics and Drug Testing." accessed May 8, 2023, https://onlinemasters.ohio.edu/blog/high-school-athletics-and-drug-testing/)

RANDY: You know it now. You didn't know it then.

RJ: Right. I didn't know it then.

RANDY: I'm sure you had no idea it was a disease. It was a total, "It's cool, let's do it," kind of thing.

RJ: Yes. And back then, I don't think anybody recognized active addiction as a disease. It was thought of as a form of choice and that you can either quit, or you don't have to quit. Now, we can relate to it a little bit more and we have groups like Brianna's Hope, which we'll get into later. But then, it wasn't like that. They had NA and AA, and those were your choices. The court system didn't see addiction as a disease. The school system didn't see that, and we didn't know it, because we weren't educated on it. So, if I could look back and say, "Hey, I wish I could do this again," I would definitely do that.

RANDY: Definitely do what?

RJ: I would step away and go in a different direction because, at fourteen, I started doing cocaine. At sixteen I decided, "Well, this is too much. I've got to drop out of school." I gave my mom an ultimatum: "Either you go sign the paperwork for me to drop out of school, or you're going to go to jail for neglect because I'm not going." That's unfortunate, and I don't laugh about it, as I put her up to that and it wasn't a good thing to do. Looking back, I wish I would have never dropped out. And I wish she just would have said, "No, I'm not signing that paper." Because two years later I ended up in jail. It was on my eighteenth birthday. So, in a matter of six years, I went from very active in sports, playing quarterback and being the highlight of the football team, to sitting in a jail cell. It was that quick.

RANDY: It's not a stumble sometimes. Sometimes it's a total fall. There's nothing gradual. It goes in a hurry. You know, we talk about six years. As you look ahead six years, it seems like a long time. But if you look back six years, that was yesterday. That was a major part of your life at that time. At eighteen—from twelve to eighteen—that's a third of your life that was already spent in that struggle, in that battle. I know it didn't end there, but that is evidently where that deep-seeded darkness was planted.

RJ: Right, and unfortunately, I missed most of my childhood because of that. I was so worried about getting high and knowing that I could go lift weights or go play football if I did this drug, that I missed so much of my childhood. I never really got to be a kid, so maybe that's why I act like a kid so much now.

RANDY: Well, we will use that excuse, anyhow, until we find out differently. So, on your eighteenth birthday, you're in jail. Was that your first incarceration?

RJ: Yes, it was. I had been in residential at the age of sixteen after I dropped out of school, but it wasn't for any criminal charges. It was just for being out past curfew several times. So, I got placed in residential. But my first incarceration was on my eighteenth birthday, in 1998. I was facing sixteen Class A misdemeanors. All of that was ranging from when I started using cocaine at fourteen to when I could actively get a checking account at sixteen and started using that to supply my habit. At eighteen, I now had to face these criminal charges, and I ended up in the system. Today, as an adult, I am still fighting that fight.

RANDY: What was the length of the charges at that point? How much time were you sentenced to?

RJ: I got lucky—at least back then I thought I was. As I look back now, I wish it would have been a little harsher of a punishment, and maybe I could have caught it. But back then I looked at it as luck. I ended up with ninety days of house arrest and paying the restitution off. I got a slap on the hand. I didn't learn anything from it.

RANDY: It didn't get your attention because the consequence of that choice wasn't that severe.

RJ: Right. I spent a night in jail, and then I was out. What can you learn from that? Not much.

RANDY: Let's move on from there into your early and mid-twenties.

RJ: Unfortunately, I didn't learn anything from that mistake, and a couple of years later I ended up catching charges for dealing. I'd gotten tipped off that they were going to raid my home, so I went on the run. I was out of state for about a year, and I decided that I was tired, and I wanted to just come back and turn myself in. I came back, but unfortunately, I did not go turn myself in. So, at the age of twenty, I was facing several felony charges ranging from forgery all the way to Class B felony burglaries in two different counties. I was looking at a substantial amount of time. Once again, I just sat in jail and didn't get anything from it. I just sat there and thought, like we always do, "God if you just let me out of here, I won't do it ever again. I promise you."

RANDY: That's bargaining.

RJ: Now that I have learned what I've learned in recovery and in my faith, I know that that wasn't the reason I ended up going home any time soon, because God doesn't bargain with you. So, I ended up in prison for about six years.

RANDY: That was over these charges?

RJ: That was over those charges, yeah. And I took a substance abuse class there. Their substance abuse class at that time was basically for time reduction. They weren't really there to teach you anything. They weren't as educated as they are now either. The chance of trying to learn how to get out and stay actively in recovery was next to nothing. You couldn't find it there. And, unfortunately, you can find drugs in there just as easily as you could on the street, so I was using the whole time I was incarcerated. When I came out, I was still in active use. I wasn't in recovery.

> "Of the 2.3 million inmates currently serving sentences in American prisons, more than 50% have a history of substance abuse and drug addiction. Prisoners that enter the system are in most cases able to immediately access drugs via extensive trafficking operations that exist in most prisons. Drugs are smuggled in to correctional facilities through the mail, by visitors, and in some cases by prison officials or guards. Due to the bleak conditions of jail or prison and the easy availability of drugs, there are few incentives for an inmate to become "rehabilitated."
>
> "Prisoners that do wish to receive treatment will in most cases not have access to it. This is due in large part to budgetary restrictions at state and federal levels that cause funding to be cut for existing drug addiction treatment programs."
>
> "This is a disturbing figure considering that when inmates who are addicted to drugs receive treatment, they are less likely to return to drug use when their sentence is complete and they are therefore less likely to commit drug related crimes."
>
> (American Addiction Centers; Recover First Treatment Center . n.d. "Drug Addiction in Prison." accessed May 8, 2023, https://recoveryfirst.org/blog/treatment/drug-addiction-in-prison)

RANDY: It wasn't any kind of rehab. It was just being removed from society. No benefit, at least in how it worked for you, right?

RJ: There was nothing that I learned from it if I can say that. Nothing positive I learned from it. I learned a lot of negative things while being incarcerated, and I found a lot more hook-ups while I was there. Unfortunately, what that ended up leading to was me getting out and I was still in active use. I didn't last very long on the streets. I ended up right back in for violations for dirty drug screens and went right back to prison. That was most of my whole twenties, from the time I turned twenty until the time I turned thirty. I was in and out, in and out, in and out. It went on even past that, but I lost my whole twenties to the penitentiary.

RANDY: Was there any kind of, "I'm tired of this. I'm sick and tired of being sick and tired," during your twenties? Was there futility?

RJ: Yeah. You know, you're so sick and tired of it when you're incarcerated. It's just when you come back out, then that sick and tired—you seem to forget what the incarceration was and how awful it was in there, and you're right back.

RANDY: You weren't sick and tired of the drug; you were sick and tired of incarceration. But until you change the root of what sent you there, there wouldn't be any change.

RJ: That ended up being the problem for several years during my twenties. I just wasn't ready to quit. And if you're not ready to quit, you're not going to accomplish it. I know that I've heard many podcasts through *Faith In Your Recovery* that explain the fact that we have to be ready. And if we're not ready, it's going to be hard for you to be able to retain recovery and keep that recovery.

RANDY: And there's no option for us to be able to push that button so you will be ready. That's got to come from within you, and just like the journey, the button is different for everyone, right?

RJ: Yeah, it's not like the Staples commercials, where you can hit that Easy Button.

RANDY: You said during your twenties you had all that struggle, the time in jail and in prison, you already talked about six years of your teen life. So up until the age of thirty, you spent most of your life bound to drugs.

RJ: Well, I mean, even past that. But, luckily, in my thirties, I found recovery. I would be there for six months or a year and then I would fall back in. I hear people use the words, "You failed," you know. "You failed this time, but you can get back up." I never use that word because failure is so permanent to me. So, I *stumbled*, and I had those stumblings all the way through until I got clean, which was September 29th, three years ago. I'm forty-one today, so it took my whole life. I still have a lot of life left in this recovery.

RANDY: We hope so. We sure hope so. You're talking about the word failure and how that's not a part of your vocabulary when it comes to your recovery, though there are those who want to use that word. I want to liken that to this: I hear somebody say, "I'm 200 days clean," or whatever the number may be. And then you hear from them a little while later and they say, "Well, I relapsed. Now I've got to start over." I don't believe you've got to start over. I've always said, if you lose thirty-five pounds and gain back fifteen, you're still twenty pounds ahead of the game. I realize that may be a weak illustration, but numerically, to me, no. You may have lost that day or that moment, but it's up to you whether you've got to go back and start over or work from where you were. You've got new tools now.

RJ: Here's the thing: how can you lose those two years? You gained those two years. That's your two years that you worked for. That's two years that you fought for. Those two years didn't go away. I agree with that. I totally agree with that, and I know there are going to be a lot of people that are going to be controversial over that, but everybody has their own opinion.

RANDY: Just like that journey—and we're not trying to convince you, but letting you know all things recovery—there are different options. So, it was in your thirties, you said, that you started to get serious and start to look at recovery. Is that when you began to experience some recovery movements or groups? Speak to that a little bit to help folks understand.

RJ: I never really found a meeting that worked for me. What I always ended up doing is I would try to do this on my own, and as we all know, doing it on your own, most of the time—I won't say all the time, because there are people that slide by on that—but it's just not feasible.

RANDY: Dr. Phil would say, "How's that working for you?" Usually, it's not working well.

RJ: That's the reason I kept having those stumbling blocks. I would try to do it on my own. Learning and looking back now and knowing you can't do this on your own, I wish I could have learned that at thirty years old. I wish I could have found a

Brianna's Hope at thirty years old, but there were no meetings like that.

RANDY: You had some Celebrate Recovery groups.

RJ: There were some CRs, yeah, but they weren't that big then. When I was younger, I grew up going to church with my mom and my grandmother. I went to a Methodist church in Muncie, Indiana. That church is huge now. I went to that church for several years, so the seed was planted as a child. I knew that the only thing that was going to work for me was some kind of faith-based recovery group if I was ever going to get clean. But unfortunately, they weren't there. So, I ended up just falling back into this same pattern of addiction and jail and prison and probation, all the way up until three and a half years ago when I landed in jail and said, "God, I'm done. Do to me whatever it is you need to do with this jail sentence. I don't really care. But I'm not going back out to this." A lot of that was because in my thirties I lost my mom too. I want to say her death was drug-induced or related because she was in active use. My dad got clean, and he's doing very well. My brother was in prison, and all of us were gone to this life of addiction. It was like our Pitman family was going to go away eventually, either by death or prison and our name was going to die out. I made a pact. I'm getting clean. I'm going to stay clean and I'm going to do whatever I can to help somebody else stay clean.

RANDY: Here's the difference I hear in what you just told us versus the bargaining from before. You went from bargaining to surrender. It was no longer what someone else could do for you, and that someone else being God. But you recognized, "I am done being the me I am now, and I am going to be the me God created me to be." Those weren't your words, obviously, but those were your thoughts, I believe.

RJ: Well, and you know, the thing about God is that He has a plan for us. And He never veers from that plan from the day He knows that we're going to be made to the day that we go home to Him, right? So, as I said, that seed was planted in me, and I just knew that I had to get back there. God gives us free will, and that free will landed me for several years in prison and jail and probation. It goes back to, "I can't do this by myself." I had to surrender, and I surrendered to my higher power. I hope that whoever hears this understands that your higher power can be God if that's what your choice is, or whatever else, but you've got to find something to make your higher power.

RANDY: To move you to that next level, I think ultimately, it's got to be God, but that's OK too.

RJ: And that's our belief, just like every Wednesday when I open a meeting up for our Brianna's Hope meeting, I tell everybody that we're a faith-based organization. But we're not going to push that on you because we want you to come as you are, and we want to love you for who you are. We hope that you get something that comes from our faith, but we just want you to be here.

RANDY: We accept you as you are, just as Jesus Christ does.

RJ: Amen

Randy: OK, so you found a connection with Brianna's Hope, and that worked for you with your faith background. The struggles were suddenly over, right? You found what you needed. There was no more temptation, no more thought of relapse. Everything worked perfectly. No flat tires on your car. No issues at work, yeah?

RJ: I don't know who you've been talking to, but....

RANDY: I thought that recovery was just an easy-peasy road.

RJ: Let me tell you that recovery is just as hard, or harder than your addiction was. The reason why I say that is because we have to work hard at this. We have to work hard at recovery every single waking moment that we have. You're always going to find something that has that temptation, or something that reflects your active use and what you did in your active use. A lot of people smoke a cigarette after they eat dinner because that's a habit formed. Well, that's the same with drugs. Every morning when I would wake up, that was the time that I made sure that I had something ready to use. That way I could get out of bed. I had to learn that I didn't need that every morning, and then I had to learn that I didn't need that every afternoon.

RANDY: What did you fill that with, then?

RJ: I filled that with.... Honestly, I filled it with devotionals there at the beginning, and that's how I did it. Whenever I woke up, I had a devotional or I had an inspirational saying that I would say out loud; an affirmation. And I would say, "I can do this today. I can do this today." I was very lucky. I had a great support system in place. When I first came into recovery, Pastor Amy, of our recovery group down in Decatur, just open-armed me, and said, "Hey, come on. I got you." She had never been a person of active use, but she understood it and she wanted to love us for who we were. I found her and then I found our drug court team that was in place down there. I figured out that our probation officers that were in place down there were regular people. When we're in our active use, and when we're in and out of jail and prison, probation officer people aren't actual people, they're somebody different. They're law enforcement. But this probation department wasn't, and they supported us for who we were.

RANDY: This was a community of people helping, a community of people supporting. And you broke down that stigma from both sides. The individuals who were using, and who were struggling with addiction started to change their attitudes towards law enforcement and the court system. Then from the other side, they viewed you as real people with an issue, with a disease, with a challenge. It wasn't the idea of "who is going to win," but "how can we all win?"

RJ: And that's how it was. It wasn't like, "Hey, when is he going to mess up so we can get him back in jail." It wasn't, "We're going to win this." It wasn't anything like that. It was, "How can we make you a better person? How can we make you succeed in life," and I loved that. I say I had the best probation officer and case manager in the world when I had Danielle Taylor. What she did for me was just amazing. I mean, she even went to the college and toured the college with me. She would go to doctor's appointments and sit with me because my fiancée would be working. Whatever the case was, she made it a point that she was going to be there to support me outside of any paycheck that she would receive from the county.

RANDY: She was involved in your life, not just your addiction struggle. She was with you and for you instead of talking about you from a distance, yes?

RJ: Yeah. And you find that with any of them up there. At that time, I didn't know that, because I only knew her. You build this trust with them, and I'd never been able to do that in all the years I'd been on probation. All through my twenties and thirties I could not form trust. As a matter of fact, I had a probation officer that told me years ago that I would never be anybody and that I would die from this disease. That came from a probation officer, so I didn't have any reason to trust any of these people.

RANDY: You'd seen nothing positive, so....

RJ: Nothing. But I openly told her that from day one I walked into her office. I said, "I will never trust you. I don't expect you to trust me. I'm a drug addict in your eyes who is never going to make it." I think that that stuck with her, and she made me out to be a liar, and I'm OK with that. Within that time, I met my fiancée. I met Tara, and we were on the same path as one another. She was on this path that she was going to be in recovery the rest of her life, and she was going to help people. And I was on the same path of forming Get Sober, Stay Sober, and being in Brianna's Hope and helping people. So, it was just a click. Right out of the gate, we learned that God has a soulmate for everybody, like you and your wife. And this was mine. We started dating and then Avenues Recovery Center opened in Fort Wayne. I had toured it with Travis, a friend of mine, and I knew that they needed help. I told Tara about it, and she was like, "I can't do this job!" And I forced her into going up there. To this day, she thanks me because she's been there now for almost two years.

RANDY: And we want to get her in here and hear her story, so leave some teasers.

RJ: Oh yeah, I don't want to get into her story too much. My point behind that is I found my support in her, and everyday support in her. So, now we've ended up on this journey together and she's doing what she's doing. And like I said, I won't go into too much detail. She got her case manager, or probation officer, from the same office that I had. We started telling each other stories about these two officers, and they're just alike. They both want us to succeed. This whole probation department has formed into nothing but, "Let's get these guys to succeed and the success rate up and everybody wins."

RANDY: It takes a village. We've got to have people on our side, and we've got to have people who challenge us as well when we need to be held accountable or we need to look in the mirror. We need someone who cares enough to say, "Hey, step back. Go take a look, and let's try it again." We've got you up to that point in your life. Are there any concerns about your past that cause you to have fears today, or have you come to a point where you have a peace where you know you can continue to move forward? Temptations? I know the temptations will always be there. It can be one and done. One time and you might fall back into it completely. Can you speak to that?

RJ: One thing I can say is don't ever get comfortable. It came to a point where I did. Probably about six to eight months ago, I got comfortable in my recovery. Maybe it was a year ago. I got comfortable in it, and I didn't fall back into using drugs. Fortunately, I didn't. Unfortunately, though, I fell back into old habits that would relate back to that.

RANDY: Behaviors from the addiction?

RJ: Yes, so luckily, I had a gentleman named Randy Davis that would put me in check on about a weekly basis, and my fiancée, of course. Luckily, by that happening, and by those people reaching out to me, I nicked that before it got to the point of relapse, or prison again, or things like that. There are always going to be temptations. There are always going to be things that come in front of us that are going to relate back to that old life. We can't sit and say that that whole old life of active addiction was horrible, because we always have our moments of laughter and good things that happened in there. But, we should have that support system in place. Because when those things do happen, if I wouldn't have had my support system in place, I wouldn't be sitting here with you today.

RANDY: I remember you and me standing—and I can almost take you back and put your feet where they were and put my feet where they were—and looking at you and saying something about you being into self-sabotage. I also remember your answer with that little chuckle and the comment, "Yeah, that's what happens in addiction." That was a kind of "Come to Jesus" moment for both of us. Take us on from there to where you are now. You've been fighting up the hill. Let's stand on the hilltop. Tell folks how life is. We've tried to make it clear; addicts do recover. Explain recovery to them as you are experiencing it.

RJ: One thing I think that we always have to recognize is we have what we call "haters." People that are going to think that we are never going to make it in life, or that we are hiding things or doing this or doing that. And what we have to do is be able to recognize that as what it is and put that to the side. I run into that a lot because I did go into self-sabotage momentarily. That one little spurt of a self-sabotage moment is something that I will probably have to live with for a few years. And that's fine. I'm OK with that. Nothing's going to be perfect. I know you want me to say that I stand on this hilltop and I'm looking down at everything that I've done. But I'll never reach that hilltop, because I'm going to work on this every single day of my life, for the rest of my life. This is like cancer. This disease is not going to ever go away. But one thing I can do is put it in remission, and that's what I've done. And that's by my faith in God and allowing Him to come into my life. I've been able to put that in remission. Today I'm very ill. My medical condition is not the greatest, but I didn't let that get me down. I made a Facebook post just a few weeks ago that said, "You know the doctor used that C word whenever I was there, but I didn't let that get me down." I still go to my meetings. I still say, "God's got this, and God's going to make this go away." He's going to make that C word go away, whether it's going home with Him and not having any pain or sitting here on this earth and continuing to help people. God's got this, man. I keep that positive outlook because if I ever veer off from a positive outlook, I know where that's going to take me, and it's going to be to the self-sabotage and self-destruction world. If I get to that point… it scares me to ever get to that point. I think that's what keeps me on the positive forefront. I'm scared to go back to that. I'm scared of the overdoses that I've had in my life. I'm scared because a very good friend of ours, Bon, who just months ago was doing great and leading CR Groups, decided to use one last time.

RANDY: RJ, I know you can't give an exact number, but ballpark, how many friends have you lost to addiction, be it alcohol or drugs or related to that?

RJ: The funny thing is I was just speaking to a high school friend not too long ago, and we started looking back at the people that are left—not the people that are gone—because the list is shorter of how many of us are left. It's a very short list, unfortunately.

RANDY: So, you've lost way too many. One is too many. We get that, but when it's over and over and over....

RJ: Yeah, it's like a continually revolving door. Unfortunately, when Covid hit, our numbers went up and....

RANDY: Isolation. That's deadly to someone in addiction.

"The addiction epidemic was already a massive problem throughout the United States. Rates of substance abuse, overdose, and more are on the rise year over year. 70,980 people died of a drug overdose in 2019, a 4.6% increase over the year before."

"Unfortunately, 2020 only made the problem worse. COVID-19 swept across the globe, sending people into a panic and forcing them into their homes. The effects of the coronavirus were far more than physical, though. High levels of stress often lead people to seek relief through alcohol and substance use."

(Peace Valley Recovery. n.d. "The Impact of Two Epidemics: Addiction and COVID-19." accessed May 8, 2023, https://www.peacevalleyrecovery.com/blog/the-impact-of-two-epidemics-addiction-and-covid-19/)

RJ: We were very fortunate in Brianna's Hope because we all came together and said, "How do we still get these meetings to people?" And, at the time I was leading the meeting here in

Portland, and we all started doing these Zoom meetings. I think that really helped our Brianna's Hope numbers not fall. I'm not saying that we have to have high numbers to be so great, but....

RANDY: But you want to be effective in reaching people.

RJ: Exactly. Because the higher our number is, the more people we're able to help. We lost a lot who had been in recovery during Covid. I would say that my life today—back to what you asked me—would be great. I love my life. I love where I'm at. I look down this—what you would call the hilltop—and I'm grateful from where I was. Because if I wouldn't have gone through all that I wouldn't be able to sit here today and reach other people. I wouldn't know or have the education that I have about this, so I'm grateful.

RANDY: Great. Hooray for you and we are thankful for that. As you know, the name of our podcast is *Faith In Your Recovery*. I often ask our guests to define that in their own words. What does that title mean to you?

RJ: It means a couple of different things, right? In my eyes, I know there are people that will disagree, but we have to have faith in the Lord in order to keep going on this path to recovery. We also have to have faith that recovery works. Here are a couple of different meanings behind that. So, I have faith in recovery working because I've seen it work. I've seen it with my own two eyes. Not just in myself, but in so many people sitting at my meetings on Thursday nights in Portland or on Wednesday nights in Decatur. That list can go on and on. I've been to about thirteen of our Brianna's Hope chapters, and I have seen many that have gone to recovery or rehab and have come back and are leading Brianna's Hope meetings now. So, I've seen it work. I have that faith in recovery, and I've always had my faith in the Lord. So, "faith in your recovery" means two different things. I have to have God and I have to know that recovery works.

RANDY: Yeah, and you just testified to the proof of both. We've got to have faith in our journey, and the list goes on. Thank you. Thank you for that answer. Anything you want to close with here, RJ?

RJ: No. I appreciate that I've been able to be here. The listeners that have sat through this and have heard it, I hope we've touched somebody with this. I hope that somebody can reach out to a support, whether it be you or anybody and try to get that guidance. And I just appreciate that and for you having me.

RANDY: Absolutely, we are so thankful for your willingness to open up. Your story is not easy to tell, but it's important to tell for yourself as well as for others. So, folks, thanks once again for joining us today on *Faith In Your Recovery*. We hope that you'll go ahead and download this. Subscribe. That's your way of clapping or saying an amen. We look forward to the next time. God Bless. Stay in the battle!

Chapter 6

Tyler Miller– "I'm not using again, period."

Tyler was a self-avowed weekend warrior that digressed into a daily user. He didn't know a better way to deal with his lack of self-worth and sense of abandonment. After a ten-to-fifteen-day blackout, he committed to a seventy-two-hour hospital stay. After a long period of "white-knuckling" his recovery, he recently celebrated one year clean from all substance use. He wants other strugglers to know that they are worth it and that there is hope.

RANDY: Our guest today is from Union City, Indiana. Over there, real close to that Ohio line, Tyler Miller. Tyler, welcome.

TYLER: Good to be here.

RANDY: Thank you. We're glad you're with us. We're going to hear Tyler's story, and I'm sure he's going to have some words that make a big impact. I don't want to steal his thunder, but I understand that you just celebrated one year clean, right?

TYLER: Yes, sir. It's a big deal.

RANDY: That is a big deal. We want to hear some of the struggle that was a major part of your life. We want to hear about the victory. We want to hear about where you're at today. Let's just jump into that and go back to those early years. Tyler, tell us what you were like, what kind of a kid you were. You're only thirty-three now but tell us of those younger years.

TYLER: I was adopted when I was young. My birth-mother was an addict and still is. She's currently in jail. My sister and I were adopted when I was about a year old. I have a younger brother who was not adopted with us, and he's currently in the same jail my mother is in right now. I was raised in a good home. I went to church. I did good in school. While I grew up, I was fine. I was a straight-A student and all that good stuff. But that self-worth thing that a lot of addicts struggle with, it ended up coming through. My addiction was in the last couple of years, and it all just came to a head.

RANDY: Tyler, if I can ask, why was there a need for the adoption? Were your biological parents just unable to raise you?

TYLER: My biological father wasn't in the picture. I mean, I know who he is. He's a good guy. But at the time, he just wasn't in the picture. And my mom was an addict. She was in and out of jail. So, she signed the rights over to my adoptive parents. I know all four of my parents. They're very good people. And it's something I've dealt with and have gotten over. There was some anger, some issues with that, but I've recovered.

RANDY: There had to be a sense of abandonment once you were old enough to recognize that.

TYLER: Yeah, there was. And when you get it in your head, it takes over. A lot of us addicts, we deal with that kind of stuff.

RANDY: I'm going to guess that even though you knew better, there were thoughts of "Did I not measure up? Did they not want me?" I'm going to guess you went through all of that.

TYLER: Yeah. And then when I got into recovery, I learned that it had nothing to do with me. It wasn't my fault. That's on them. It's not me.

RANDY: You may have had to pay some of the consequences of all of that, but you certainly didn't create that.

TYLER: Right. And I reconciled with my mother after thirty years. I forgave her for all of that, and now we are okay. But being that she's still in addiction, that's something I can't be a part of right now. I mean, I still talk to her and stuff, but there are certain people, places, and things that you have to get away from once you start doing the right thing. When you're not getting high anymore, you start veering. People don't come around you and stuff like that.

When I got clean, I was still able to be around people that were in addiction, and that was part of how I could be an example to them. I was able to be around them and still not use. A lot of people can't do that, but I could.

RANDY: OK. Let's go from those early childhood years to once you got out of high school. Let's look at the part of your life when your heavy drug usage started. I'm guessing that's probably going to be your twenties. Tell us who you were in those years.

TYLER: Well, in my twenties, I was married, and I started having kids. I have four boys. My marriage was good. We were young. I got married right out of high school. Stuff happens and you have lots of ups and downs. You grow and things happen. When I was nearly thirty-one, we split. I got a divorce. Then, I was with another girl, and I got my heart broken. That's when the addiction came.

RANDY: That's where the spiral started. OK, I'm going to go ahead and ask you a tough question here. What was it that finally was the last straw in your first marriage?

TYLER: The other girl.

RANDY: OK. Thanks for your honesty. We appreciate that. Folks, as you can tell, this is raw and it's one of those things where Tyler is, as we said earlier, just now a year clean. This is all pretty fresh. Let's hear about that moment you mentioned. It was a heartache and a heartbreak that kind of started you downhill. Tell us what those steps were like, what they entailed, how you got started, and your drugs of choice or drugs of doom.

TYLER: When I was about twenty years old, I dabbled in it, and thought, "This is fun." There was nothing connected to it like cocaine. I was just doing it for fun. I wasn't addicted to it. And I put it down, like, "No more," you know? So, there was no trauma attached to it or anything like that.

RANDY: It didn't create an issue?

TYLER: Yeah, it was a good time. It was like, "Hey, I like this. I'm going fast! Woohoo!" But I just put it down. Fast forward ten years and I come to this heartbreak. Major trauma. And a seed was planted in my head. I was thinking, "But you could relapse. There's a chance you could relapse." And that was it. That was all.

Words are very powerful. That got in my head on top of the heartbreak. "OK, I'm not good enough. I could relapse. This is all I am. Ten years removed from my usage. This is all I am?" So, yeah.

RANDY: What were you turning to at that point?

TYLER: I went to meth. And, you know, I often thought I could be a "weekend warrior." I thought, "I'll just do it on the weekend. I'll be all right." People told me, "Don't do it. It's not going to work out for you. It ain't going to be good." And it wasn't. A weekend turns into, "Oh we can do a little bit more. We'll be OK. More will be OK."

RANDY: Suddenly, it was a three-day weekend. Suddenly, it went from three days to four and so on.

TYLER: It started affecting my body. I lost weight. I started to get real paranoid. The thing about methamphetamine is that if you have any trauma, any mental trauma coming on, or going on, you should never use that drug. It's psychosomatic. It takes your mind, and it just twists it and turns it in on itself. It's not good.

> "Methamphetamine (meth) is a synthetic stimulant that is addictive and can cause considerable health adversities that can sometimes result in death. Meth can be smoked, snorted, injected, or taken orally and is often used with other substances."
>
> "Meth not only changes how the brain works, but also speeds up the body's systems to dangerous, sometimes lethal, levels—increasing blood pressure and heart and respiratory rates. People who repeatedly use meth may also experience anxiety, paranoia, aggression, hallucinations, and mood disturbances."
>
> (Substance Abuse and Mental Health Services Administration. n.d. "Learn about Methamphetamine." accessed May 10, 2023, https://www.samhsa.gov/meth)

RANDY: How often were you using then?

TYLER: Oh, man. When I was going, it was every day.

RANDY: Multiple times in a day?

TYLER: Yeah. And then the longest I stayed up was six days in a row. That was the longest for me. No sleep; not eating, not drinking. I mean, that would make you go loopy.

RANDY: Yes. Physically, emotionally, and mentally.

TYLER: Everything. And I was still dealing with the heartbreak, you know, and from the divorce too. I was dealing with the guilt from what I had done to my ex-wife with the cheating thing. And, then with my sons, of course. I broke the family up, so I had to deal with that. The guilt. But you've got to forgive yourself for it.

RANDY: Your coping tool was meth at that time, yes?

TYLER: Yes.

RANDY: You told us that you used it multiple times, just about every day. How were you able to score that meth? How were you able to afford it? Were you still working? Were you able to function on a job, or did you have to turn to other means?

TYLER: I was still working at the time, and I lost one job because of it. People were noticing that I wasn't quite myself anymore. It ended up that I got a bad batch, and I ended up breaking out really bad and they noticed that, but also my demeanor was different. I was losing weight and I just wasn't myself. I failed a drug test at work, and they fired me. I got clean for about a month after that. I got a new job and thought, "Hey, everything's going well, you know. And, uh, cool, I'm clean and feeling good." And then, I wasn't quite done with it.

RANDY: What drew you back to it? Did someone offer it to you? Did you go on a search?

Tyler: I got with a girl who offered it to me, and I did it. Then it got worse. You know, most people say if they do it again after they've stopped for a while, they're going to do it worse. And I did. I went bad. I mean, I got strung all the way out and it got bad. I ended up having a car crash because I fell out a couple of days before Christmas. That was in 2020.

RANDY: That accident, was that a single-car accident?

TYLER: It was just me. I was the only person. That totaled my car and I had to get a rental. After that, it was just the drugs.

That Christmas I was just falling out. I just wasn't myself, you know.

RANDY: OK. So, you lost one job because you were spiraling, then you had the accident. Take us to the next step.

TYLER: I got another job, and I ended up losing that one, too.

RANDY: For the same reasons?

TYLER: Well, what happened with this one was I had a concussion from the car crash. And when you have a concussion, you're not supposed to use. I did and ended up having ten days where I didn't remember anything. I went into this mini coma thing or whatever. Nobody knew where I was at. I didn't know what I was doing. I was using at the time, and I just went into this... I don't know what it was. I mean, I woke up ten days later thinking that it was still December 23rd, but it was like January 9th or something like that. That's how I lost the other job.

RANDY: So, you were blacked out for ten days? Like a bender?

TYLER: Yeah, I was just gone. Nobody knew where I was. I didn't know what I was doing, and I can't really remember. Bits and pieces of it came back, but I still can't put it all together to this day.

RANDY: How do you feel about that, now, as you look back at it? You've got to feel lucky to be alive.

TYLER: Yeah. I mean, of course. The car crash could have killed me.

RANDY: Absolutely. And then the concussion and the use of meth on top of that.

TYLER: It was dangerous, but I wasn't done with it. I ended up going to Reid Hospital. It has an inpatient where you can go and it's a rehab and mental hospital.

RANDY: For psychological purposes? Reid Hospital is in Wayne County, right?

TYLER: I went there for three days, and that was the beginning of my getting clean. I knew I was getting clean there. I went there because I wanted to get my memory back because I thought I was crazy.

RANDY: And did you go there by choice?

TYLER: Yeah. I went there by choice. I did three days, and I got clean.

RANDY: A seventy-two-hour hold of a sort.

TYLER: But it wasn't. They couldn't hold me. It was voluntary. Then, at the end of that, I came out and I was good. From that point, I decided, I'm not doing this anymore.

RANDY: So, was that your last usage?

TYLER: Yeah.

RANDY: Were you just sick and tired of being sick and tired? Is that what made you make that decision, or did you just want to find "you" again?

TYLER: I went in there. I was in a room, and I was scared.

RANDY: A solitary room by yourself?

TYLER: There were like a couple more patients in there. We were on rollouts and stuff like that. But it was just the feeling that I was all alone, and I was scared. I was paranoid, of course, because I was coming down off the drug. And I was like, "I can't do this again. I can't do it." Of course, I was missing my sons, and I was like, "I just can't do this." From there on, I said, "No, I'm not going back to this paranoid state. I'm not doing this. I'm not putting myself in this again." I mean, I was weak. I lost my mind. The drugs had made me lose my mind. That was a bad thing for me.

RANDY: Had people been trying to get you to go for help or was this just you knowing that it wasn't going well, and you needed help?

TYLER: A lot of people didn't say a lot to me. But, when I lost a couple of jobs, some said, "You need to go get some help for this," and stuff like that. But you're not going to do it unless you want to.

RANDY: Exactly. Did you have anybody kind of rooting for you?

TYLER: I did. My sister, my dad, and my family. They didn't say a whole lot, but they did at the same time, you know?

RANDY: They didn't have to say a lot, but you knew what they meant by a few words?

TYLER: Yeah. It was like that because when you're in addiction, it's a shameful thing. They don't want to talk about it, and you don't want to talk about it. You all don't want to talk about it. And if they say something to you, you're going to be defensive because you're insecure about it, you know? And they don't want that either. It's really got to be something you want to do. You have to want to get clean, you know? Then there's no fight with anything. There's just a fight with yourself. You say, "I want to get clean, and now I'm going to do it. I don't care." And that's where I'm at today. Today, I don't care what happens. I'm not getting high again.

RANDY: OK. There you are. You've just spent seventy-two hours trying to get your head together and trying to get your life together, and you decide during that time that you're done. Give us the next step of how that worked for you and how you've moved forward.

TYLER: After all that, I spent about a month where I hardly interacted with anybody, like nobody. Because, I just didn't want to, you know?

RANDY: You were still trying to find yourself.

TYLER: Yeah, I just didn't want to mess with anybody. Because, for one, I was still scared from coming out of the psych hold. That's a scary thing. And I was still trying to figure out what I was going to do. There were my sons. I just had a lot of things going on. I still had my apartment, but I didn't have a job. I didn't have a car. I just kept thinking, "What am I going to do?" I was just stuck in this kind of state. I was just scared.

RANDY: Well, that's a transition time. It makes total sense because you were not clear enough of mind to make the best choice for you then.

TYLER: Right. And I was dealing with the emotions that I was trying to mask with the drug because the drug would make your mind go fast. It's fast. And you would be aggressive in everything that you were kind of feeling. If you were thinking of something, immediately 10,000 other things would come to mind.

RANDY: You bet. And then you started to feel things you hadn't in a long time.

TYLER: Yeah. As you get out of it, you have to have a change of mindset. As I am starting to build my self-confidence back, I am asking myself, "What am I going to do? What are my next steps?" But I was "white knuckling." Do you know that term?

RANDY: Absolutely but go ahead and explain it to other folks.

TYLER: So, "white knuckling" is when you're not doing anything like meetings or anything like that. You're just not using. You're clean, but you're not doing anything else to help. You're just staying clean, and that's not really the best way to go about it. You need a support group. You need somebody who knows what they're talking about.

"White knuckling can be a dangerous way to try to stay sober because it sets you up for failure. If you're not getting help and support from others in recovery, you're more likely to relapse. Recovery is a process that takes time, effort, and commitment. Trying to go it alone is often not successful."

"If you're struggling with the urge to white knuckle, there are things you can do to overcome it. First, reach out for help and support from others in recovery. There are many resources available to you, including 12-step programs, therapy, support groups, and treatment centers, just like ours. Getting help from others will give you the strength and courage you need to stay sober."

"Second, make sure you're taking care of yourself physically and emotionally. Addiction can take a toll on your body and mind, so it's important to nurture yourself with healthy habits like exercise, relaxation, and healthy eating. Taking care of yourself will help reduce the urge to white knuckle and will make sobriety more sustainable in the long-term."

(Plum Creek Recovery Ranch. n.d. "What Does White Knuckling in Sobriety Mean." accessed May 10, 2023, https://plumcreekrecoveryranch.com/what-does-white-knuckling-in-sobriety-mean)

RANDY: At that point, had you talked to your family and told them what was going on? Did they believe you? Because there had probably been some ups and downs with your stories. But had you told them at that point that you were done?

TYLER: Yeah.

RANDY: How did they respond?

TYLER: All of them were like, "Great!" That's what they wanted. They never wanted to see me walk down that path. None of my four parents did. They supported me 100 percent.

RANDY: You said you had those thirty days of self-imposed isolation or being by yourself. Tell us about day thirty-one, so to speak.

TYLER: Kevin Lawrence contacted me at one point. I kind of fought him off the first time he contacted me. I'm sitting there, and I'm like, "Man, I've got to do something else. You know, I need a life coach." Because I was just sitting there, and I was spinning. I was like, "I don't know what I'm doing." I got a hold of Kevin and this time I said, "I need a life coach because I don't know where I'm going from here, and I need somebody." I knew how Kevin was when he was coaching my boys, so....

RANDY: Explain that to folks who don't know.

TYLER: OK. Kevin, he's hard-nosed, you know? He's like, "You need to do this, you need to do that." And he was usually right when he was coaching kids and wrestling. He would say, "No, you do it this way. Just do it this way." I was an athlete, so being coached is something I needed.

RANDY: You needed directions.

TYLER: I needed something. I needed directions. I needed somebody to go, "Boom. You need to do this right here." I like to argue, so I needed somebody that would say no. That's a part of it for me. That's what I needed. That might not go well with somebody else, but for me, that's what I needed. I needed somebody like that to be right there, and he did it for me. I invited him over to my house, and I started talking about a couple of things. He was there from that night forward. It was a different mindset.

"A support system is a network of people who provide practical or social support. There are broadly two types of support systems: those geared toward personal relationships or recovery."

"Personal support systems may include:
- family members and relatives
- friends
- neighbors
- members of organizations you're a part of, like churches or clubs"

"For personal support systems, it may be a good idea to spend a little time thinking about the people in your life whom you trust as a source of support."

"Recovery support systems are groups designed specifically for those in substance use disorder recovery, such as:
- 12-step programs
- recovery and treatment programs
- in-person and virtual support groups"

"Some people might choose to only use recovery support systems on a short-term basis during their active recovery. Others may incorporate recovery support systems into their lives for many years."

"There's no right or wrong way to approach finding support from others during recovery and sobriety. It's all about trying different things and discovering what works best for you."

(PsychCentral. n.d. "What is a support system?" accessed May 12, 2023, https://psychcentral.com/addictions/the-importance-of-good-support-systems-in-sobriety#what-are-support-systems)

RANDY: Do you remember anything that he said that really caused the lights to come on?

TYLER: Actually, he said something to me, and looking back at it, it was like the smartest thing ever. He said, "I have something in my pocket, and you can have it. Whatever it is, you can have it, but I need you to tell me what it is." He pulls it out and he's like, "What is it?" I said, "Cocaine." I didn't want to do meth again because you get loopy, but when I was on cocaine, I was having fun, right? So, I said cocaine. After that, we talked a little bit more and he left. A light bulb came on. I thought, "I don't have a car. I don't have a job. I should have asked for his car keys. I should have asked for money, not cocaine, right?" That was a light bulb for me. It was like, "Boom!" So, I texted him and said, "I like how you just played in my head right there a little bit." It got me thinking, and that was it. I should have been thinking about anything else that would have been better for my life other than that. That was the moment I struggled with whether I was an addict or not. Because I really thought the cocaine I used back when I was in my twenties was just for having fun. So, at that moment right there, I realized I'm an addict.

RANDY: When he pulled his hand out of his pocket and said, "You can have this if you can tell me what it is." You said cocaine instead of saying something that would benefit you. That was the switch?

TYLER: That was the switch right there. The light bulb went on like that, dude.

RANDY: What was the next play between you and Kevin? Folks, Kevin's one of our chapter leaders of A Better Life - Brianna's Hope. He is in the Union City, Indiana area. We are a faith-based, compassion-filled, participant-driven, support and recovery movement for those battling with substance abuse disorder/addiction. Kevin's ABLBH group is where Tyler is from, and they have a long-term connection through school. Kevin has that skill of still hanging in there and pulling for people. He's a great supporter. Tyler, tell us about the next step between you and Kevin or your journey towards sobriety and being clean.

TYLER: My next step... my clean date is January 14th. OK, so, everybody knows the difference between a recovery date and a clean date. A recovery date is when you start putting the work in. My first step of work was February 14th, Valentine's Day. Ha! Instead of going out with somebody, I went to my first meeting at Brianna's Hope on February 14, 2021. My first meeting was on Valentine's Day.

RANDY: You know what? Without getting too mushy, that's showing love for yourself.

TYLER: That's a good point because it's all about yourself. It's all about you.

RANDY: You've said that over and over. You know, everybody can want it for you. But until you want it....

TYLER: Self-love is one of the things you have to have. It has to be about that. You do it for yourself. No other reason. There's no other reason out there. My children, yes, but if I'm not good with myself, I'm not good for them.

RANDY: Tell us about that first meeting.

TYLER: OK. It was at Wesleyan United Methodist Church. It was down in the basement. I was religious growing up and stuff like that, but I'm kind of falling off with that stuff. So, that was kind of nerve-racking, going back into church.

RANDY: It's scary.

TYLER: A little bit. And then I was going to a Brianna's Hope meeting, which is scary itself. I had to walk down these stairs to the basement, and that was even a little bit scarier. I thought, "What am I getting myself into?" But I got down there and the people there were supporters or other addicts or people that aren't even addicts. But they are just there to learn about it because they've had family members addicted or something else. I started listening to it, and I started listening to other people's stories, and some of the lessons they went through and stuff like that. And I just started applying it to my life. A lot of people will go into NA, but Brianna's Hope is not an NA. At NA, they go through the twelve steps and all that and they work through it. I didn't need to do that. Life put me through the twelve steps naturally.

107

RANDY: I've never heard that phrase. I like that. "Life put me through the twelve steps."

TYLER: It did. I looked at the twelve steps and I thought, "This all happened to me already." I didn't get it. But I'm not going to say don't go to NA, because that's a great support system. Any support system you can get is a good one.

RANDY: That's a good comment.

TYLER: But that's just how my recovery happened. I think I missed three meetings in a year, two of them because of work.

RANDY: Now, these meetings are weekly.

TYLER: Every Sunday night.

RANDY: Basically, fifty-two in a year. Of course, weather might cancel them, or something else. But you only missed three in a year. You must have been serious about recovery.

TYLER: The Sunday night one is the only one I can make because I work the night shift, 7:30 p.m. to 5:30 a.m. Meetings are on Sunday nights, and my night shift doesn't start until Monday night. Even if I have to work overtime, and we work on a Sunday, it doesn't start until 9:00. The meetings start at 6:30 and run till 8:00, so I'm good. I can still make it.

RANDY: That's awesome. Tell us a little more about your involvement and any other steps or resources you may have used or people you may have relied upon to help you get to where you are today.

TYLER: I have a group of friends that I relied on, that I could talk to and stuff. Kevin was the heavy one. He was kind of a sponsor in a way. He wasn't an official sponsor, but he was kind of my sponsor.

RANDY: He was your go-to guy.

TYLER: Yeah. If I needed to have support, I would reach out to someone. If that person wasn't there, I would reach out to this person, this person, or this person. He was my main guy though. And, as I got further along, it was like every day I was talking to him, asking him how he was doing. He was asking me how I was doing, you know, those kinds of things. Then it started dwindling off because I wasn't needing him as much. I needed him just to kind of keep me steady. He did a great job, and now others look to me when they need help.

RANDY: How does that make you feel?

TYLER: It's neat, really. It's different. I didn't have experiences with some of the drugs like heroin, fentanyl, or opiates. I don't have experience with those, so some of those I can't really relate to. But I can help with self-love and understanding. I can be there and say, "You need to stay away from this, stay away from that," and just be a support. If somebody needs help, they can talk to me because I understand it. Empathy is a big deal. I can understand what they're going through. I fought through the triggers, too. I had triggers early on. I don't anymore. That's the thing. It's all about thinking.

RANDY: You keep that attitude and be careful because one of those triggers may sneak up on you. And you've just got to be ready to kick it to the back.

TYLER: Oh, yeah, you just have to say, "No I'm not going to…."

RANDY: And then stand on it.

TYLER: Exactly. That's the thing. I've said I'm not going to, and I'm not going to. And there are certain reasons for that. I'm an example to many different people. If they see me use, they might be like, "Well, you know, he's doing it again."

RANDY: You don't just let down yourself. You let down the village and the community groups. Let me ask you a tough question here. You've gotten to this point in your recovery, a little over a year clean. Have you gone back and taken care of any of the damage your addiction has done? Mainly, I'm talking about your relationships. Where are you with your kids? Share that with us. I know that may be tough, but folks need to hear it.

TYLER: I was completely honest with my sons.

RANDY: How old are they now?

TYLER: My oldest is fourteen. He's a freshman in high school. Then I have a thirteen-year-old, an eleven-year-old, and a nine-year-old. All are boys.

RANDY: That's a handful! Tell us about your relationship with them.

TYLER: It's good. There was the divorce and all that, and, you know, I'm kind of hard-nosed. I'm blunt. I don't let them get away with things. I have great examples of what drugs can do to a person to tell them about. I have a brother sitting in jail right now. I have a mother sitting in jail right now.

RANDY: Are both of those drug-related situations?

TYLER: My brother has been in and out of jail, juvie, and prison since he was thirteen years old.

RANDY: Is he younger or older than you?

TYLER: Younger. He's thirty years old, and he's a great example of what could happen at a young age if you go down the wrong path. Kevin told me this, and it was something good. He said now that I've gone through it, if one of my sons does go down that path, I can help them. I'll know exactly what to do. And that's a big deal.

RANDY: You're going to have that empathy that you just spoke about because you know the damage it did to you physically, emotionally, relationally, all of that. And, if you've got a son doing that, you're going to know what he's doing. You're also going to know what to say to stay close to him and love him without enabling and crossing that line. I don't see you as the kind that would enable. I will tell you that Tyler.

TYLER: No, I won't. But I'll know if they're doing it. They'll want to hide but I'll be able to see it. It's just one of those things I can pinpoint because I've seen all the signs. It's like, "Been there, done that."

RANDY: Where are you at this point with your mom and your brother? Do you speak?

TYLER: I do, but them being high is just one of the things I can't be around. I just can't. It's an arm's reach relationship right now. I still care about them a lot, and I still love him, but I have to keep it within arm's reach. It's just one of those things that could easily turn the other way if I'm not careful, and I could become involved in something I don't want to be involved in.

RANDY: You're thirty-three, right? Speak to all the thirty-three-year-olds out there who are where you were, who are struggling in the battle right now, who are dealing with their own

110

addiction. Give them some advice and show them a little light to help them take the first step or the next step toward recovery.

TYLER: You're worth it. There's always hope. There's help. If you want it, there's help. Somewhere out there, there is help. In every town there is something, and you're not alone. You're not the only one that's dealing with it. A lot of people are.

RANDY: I'm going to ask you to add one more thing to that simply because of what you said earlier. Recognize your addiction. When Kevin pulled that out of his pocket and made that comment, that's when you realized, "Wow. I've been fighting this battle and I recognize it, and I need to reach out." So, recognize and reach. That's a couple of good Rs right there.

TYLER: Recognize and reach out. There are people out there that won't look down on you and will recognize that you are fighting a battle and will help you.

RANDY: How many people are you around now that recall the Tyler of that time in addiction? And do they see you now and go, "Man, I can see a difference, a real change."

TYLER: There are a lot of people, even addicts. They'll just say, "That's awesome, that's great. You keep doing what you're doing." That's the big reason why I keep doing what I'm doing now. It's not just about me. It's about them because they look at me and say, "If he can do it, maybe I can too." And because most of them know who my family is, they're like, "If he can do it, then we can." That's a big deal to me. That's a big deal in my community because I was known very well for the wrong reasons. Both sides of my family are known very well around town. I was a coach and stuff too. So, me doing this and coming up out of it is a big deal.

RANDY: You know what? It works both ways. When you are recognized and known the fall seems greater. But because you were recognized and known and you've made the climb, it makes your story go even farther. You know, people sometimes love to see you in misery. But to see you in success, they've got to be nodding their heads going, "There is hope." As we say, hashtag, "addicts do recover." You're living proof of that. How do you want to continue to help those who are struggling?

TYLER: We do recover. I have my messenger app. Certain people have my phone numbers and stuff like that. And I keep going to the meetings as an example to anybody else that walks in the door. I want them to know that they can do it because I'm young, you know, and it can be done. Of course, I still have issues.

RANDY: We all do.

TYLER: I've got problems like everybody, even just walking through life. There are bills and this and that and all the other things. We've all got stuff that's going on. Today it's freaking snowing outside. Who likes that? Nobody! That puts a damper on my day right there. It's cold.

RANDY: Interesting question. You made the comment when you went to that first meeting on February 14th of 2021, it was kind of tough to even walk down those steps at the church. How do you feel in the church now?

TYLER: Oh, I don't really go to the services and stuff. But now going to the meetings is nothing. I just walk down in there. And, if I'm not there, I'm getting a phone call. I usually let Kevin know if I'm not going to be there. But that hasn't been many times. But if I'm not there it's like, "Hey, what's going on?"

RANDY: It seems you got over that stigma in a hurry.

TYLER: Oh, yeah.

RANDY: I want folks to hear that.

TYLER: Yeah. Just because it's in the church, don't let that stop you. The meeting is the meeting and that's what we're doing.

RANDY: Yeah, we're faith-based, not faith-forced, not faith-expected. That doesn't mean we won't share our faith, but we're going to let you be where you're at. We'll trust God to take you where you need to be.

TYLER: Yeah.

RANDY: What about your last word of advice? Is there anything you would like to say to anyone from your past? That brings up a thought. How many friends would you guess you have lost to addiction over the years, Tyler? Overdose deaths or alcohol-related accidents.

TYLER: That's the thing. I've not lost anybody.

RANDY: Seriously?

TYLER: None of my friends died, but I've seen them OD. I've known of people that died, but I haven't had anyone close to me that has died from that. I've had my uncle and my grandma pass away just this last year. That was a big deal for me. I've seen overdoses from my brother and a couple of other friends right in front of me, and it's scary. But I haven't had anything like that.

RANDY: Good.

TYLER: That's a tough one.

RANDY: Listen, congratulations. Don't let the journey stop here today. I once heard it said that we didn't come this far to only come this far. You know, we celebrate that one year of being clean.

TYLER: That's why I thank you for letting me come on this podcast. This is bigger than what I was doing.

RANDY: Right. We'd like to bring you back for year two. We want to hear about where recovery is then and where that clean date is. And another thing, there's a difference between getting clean and getting clear. Clean simply means I've stopped using. Getting clear is a matter of being able to function and getting rid of some of those addictive behaviors, and you're getting there.

TYLER: Right. It's a mindset. You have to have the mindset. It doesn't matter what goes on in my life, I'm not going to use. I mean, everybody's got bad days, and everybody's got this and that, but I'm not going to use, period.

RANDY: Awesome. Good closing words for you. You're not going to use, period.

TYLER: Yes.

RANDY: We'll let that be that. Once again, Tyler, thanks for your willingness to be vulnerable, to be real, to be raw, to share with us. To let us know that not only do addicts recover, but that you have recovered, and you continue to walk that journey. Keep it up. God bless and thanks. I know you're going to be there fighting for others. And folks, that's why we're here. It's about all things addiction. We recognize that no two journeys are the same. Nobody's going to take the same path. But we also recognize that your recovery, your clean time, can begin today. Let it begin today. Take that first step. Recognize your issue. Reach out. And if nothing else, please join us for our next episode, because it could start there or just around the next corner. Take care God bless.

Chapter 7

Jackie Sheridan— "If you let me survive this, I'll never touch drugs again."

"I can do all these things through Him who gives me strength. (Philippians 4:13 NIV)

Jackie weaves her story of sexual abuse, rape, family mental health issues, drugs, and the tragic death of her brother into a final moment of peace and hope that will speak to your heart. Drugs affected Jackie from birth. Her mom struggled with addiction and mental health issues. Jackie had her own challenges with just about every drug. She lost her brother, Gary Wade McCowan, to overdose in 2015. Gary was a father, a loving person, a veteran, and more. Jackie shares her story of trying to reach her brother before it was too late. One of the hardest things she ever had to do was leave the brother she loved so much to experience homelessness. This story is one you won't soon forget.

RANDY: We have a good friend here with us. She's going to tell us her story and touch on the story of her brother as well. Jackie Sheridan, welcome to *Faith In Your Recovery*.

JACKIE: Well, howdy. Thank you.

RANDY: It's good to have you with us. Glad you're here. Did you have a safe drive over from the big state of Ohio?

JACKIE: Yeah, I sure did. It's a little colder than I would have liked today. But hey, no snow and ice, so I'm good.

RANDY: Jackie, you and I have been friends for a long time. We've experienced a lot of different things together. But I know in your personal life you've experienced a lot as well. I want you to share with the folks who you were and what you were about in your early years.

JACKIE: Oh wow. Well, I was a very different person then than what I am now. I experienced a lot of childhood trauma. We grew up in Western Jay County, and my mother battled addiction and mental illness. There were a lot of drugs in our house. There were a lot of people in and out of our house. I was molested for years, and when that came out, nothing was ever done about it. It was one of those things where you just keep your mouth shut because "What would the neighbors think?" As I got a little bit older, the nightmares got too much for me and I started using. It was easy. I didn't have to go anywhere. I could just go right into my mom's bedroom, where she had a lot of prescription pills. I started drinking on top of that. It was ugly. I got to a point in my early years where I wasn't sober a single day. I was always drunk or high.

RANDY: I know that you've talked before about the trauma that you had to go through and how easy it was at home to obtain those drugs. But I also know you had those times when you didn't dare go inside the house. Tell the folks a little about that.

JACKIE: Yeah, absolutely. Growing up there were husbands and boyfriends, or whatever. There were drugs dealt out of our house, right off the kitchen table. There were times when I would get off the school bus and it didn't matter what the weather was, whether it was minus twenty degrees or storming. If there was a certain car in the driveway, I didn't go in. I knew that from an early age because anything could go wrong during a drug deal. We would just sit out there and wait. It wasn't anything we talked about. I knew from a very young age that I didn't discuss this with anyone. It was just something we lived with.

RANDY: It is just the way it was, right?

JACKIE: Yeah, absolutely. It was just part of our life. And to be honest, I was much older when I finally realized, "Hey, this isn't normal. Most people don't live like this."

RANDY: I know you battled some issues there. You've already said that those adverse childhood experiences, that trauma, is what led you to some of your challenges and your addiction. Share that with folks, please.

JACKIE: After being molested for years, I was a very quiet person. I kept to myself. I didn't want anyone in my bubble. I started using, and then I started partying. The partying got worse, and I ended up putting myself in a situation I couldn't get out of. I was partying with people much older than myself. I snuck out one night, and I was drunk and high as normal.

RANDY: How old were you at this time, Jackie?

JACKIE: I was fifteen, and I snuck out of my house and ended up at a party. I was raped. But I already knew nobody cared, and nobody was going to do anything about it. So, I just kept my mouth shut. I just started smoking more weed, doing more pills, and drinking more liquor until it was just constant, and I was not sober.

RANDY: Internalizing all of that, drugs became your way to at least numb it.

JACKIE: It gave me an escape. When you're high, when you're drunk, you don't feel. You don't think. You just exist. And that's what I needed to survive at that time. I never really learned how to live. I just learned how to survive.

"It's estimated that one in 13 males and one in four females are sexually abused during childhood. Being sexually abused is a childhood trauma that puts people at increased risk for substance use disorders."

"Sexual abuse is considered an adverse childhood experience (ACE). The more ACEs, the greater vulnerability to alcohol addiction or drug addiction. Some research has found that sexual abuse as an ACE is one of the strongest predictors of future substance abuse."

"People who experience child abuse of any kind, may drink alcohol or use drugs as coping mechanisms. This can be a way to self-medicate the emotions and difficulties that stem from an ACE. Using substances to mask these issues can quickly lead to drug or alcohol dependence."

(Footprints to Recovery. n.d. "The Link Between Sexual Assault, Sexual Abuse, and Addiction" accessed May 21, 2023, https://footprintstorecovery.com/blog/sexual-assault-and-addiction)

RANDY: You've said before that you moved around quite a bit during that time, from school to school, yes?

JACKIE: Yes. By the time I was in the second grade, I think I'd already been to about eight different schools, because the money went to pay for drugs instead of rent or electricity or food. I've said it many times; if it hadn't been for my grandparents, we would have gone hungry. We would've been homeless.

RANDY: Then you move into those early teen years—that thirteen, fourteen, fifteen range—and you start stepping out and going in the wrong direction.

JACKIE: I sure did. That was my life. That was the life around me. Everybody that I was around was doing the exact same thing that I was doing. It wasn't like I thought it was wrong or not normal. It was my way of coping. It was my way of just trying to deal with everything that was happening.

RANDY: In your circle, that was the accepted and normal behavior.

JACKIE: Absolutely. Like I said, everybody around me— family, friends—were all doing the exact same thing.

RANDY: If I go back and talk to one of your teachers from that day and age, how would they have described you?

JACKIE: Most of them probably would have said I was very quiet and kept to myself. I wasn't really noticed. I probably had one teacher in high school who got to see a little bit of a different version. She was very supportive and very encouraging. But again, no one knew what was going on in my day-to-day life. Nobody had a clue. I didn't talk about it.

RANDY: Was there a drug you didn't use?

JACKIE: No, there wasn't. You've got to remember back to the late 80s and early 90s, that's when crack was just coming out. I was terrified of that. I hadn't used that. I had gotten a hold of some weed that was laced. That night is truly what changed my life.

RANDY: Tell us about that.

JACKIE: My girlfriend and I had gone out to celebrate my birthday. We were going to party to get drunk and high.

RANDY: Which birthday?

JACKIE: This was my seventeenth birthday and we had gotten ahold of a joint that was laced with LSD. We didn't know that until later, and I ended up hallucinating for almost forty-eight hours. It was traumatic. It was life changing for me. I didn't really know God at that point in my life. My dad had attempted to take us to church when we were younger. But let's be real. When I was little, I would just count the lights or poke at my brother. I remember thinking—and I remember saying out loud—"If you let me survive this, I'll never touch drugs again. I will break this cycle and I will change, and I will live a life that I'm proud of." I never touched them again after that.

RANDY: You were honest to your word at that point. There are a lot of folks who want to bargain with God. But when they get what they ask for, they forget what they promised to fulfill as part of the payback.

JACKIE: Yeah, we've all seen it. But for me, that truly scared me to death. That night I thought I was going to die. I was way too young, and I just knew that I wanted a better life. I knew that I deserved it, and I knew at that point that this wasn't normal. There was more to life than this. And I worked hard. That addiction gene doesn't ever go away. You still battle that your whole life. It was still there. I had the urges and the cravings and there were even more traumatic years to come that would push me to the brink. But no, I didn't use again.

RANDY: After that marijuana being laced with LSD, that was the moment that changed your future, even though there were still struggles ahead.

JACKIE: Yes, my life completely changed. I still had to deal with the demons. I still had to deal with my nightmares. But I knew that if I could get away from where I was living and if I could get away from that perception of what I felt that everybody saw when they saw me… I always felt when people would look at me, they would just see this raggedy redhead from the wrong side of the tracks. Whether they knew my story or part of my story, or thought they knew, I always felt like people were looking down on me. I knew I needed to walk away from that to create something better for myself.

RANDY: And you probably had some paranoia. Even when looking at those who had no idea who you were, you would look at them thinking they knew that story was written on your forehead for them to read.

JACKIE: Yeah. I felt like I just had like this big imaginary sign above my head, "Hey, here's this trashy little drug-addicted ho-bag that is never going to amount to anything."

RANDY: You made mention there how you felt like you needed to get away, and I know that means physically or geographically. Tell us about that.

JACKIE: I got this amazing opportunity. My dad knew that things were bad for me. He wanted better for me. He gave me the opportunity for an open-ended ticket to Florida right after I graduated, and I took that. I had a suitcase full of clothes. I had 300 bucks on me, and I went to Florida. I ended up finding a job, and I started working full-time right away. I met my now-husband and started a new life. I just never came back home for a few years.

RANDY: That doesn't always work, but obviously it worked for you. I know that there were still challenges, problems, and trauma ahead. Go ahead with that.

JACKIE: Yeah. I moved away. It was the hardest thing. It was the hardest choice for me because I had a younger brother, Gary Wade. We were best friends. I always remember taking care of him, at a very young age. Again, my mother battled addiction. She battled her mental illness, and looking back now I realize she did the best she could at the time. I didn't feel that way then, though. I always knew I had to take care of him, so leaving him was super hard. We were only fifteen or eighteen months apart in age, so we were super close. It was just the two of us, and I had always taken care of him. But I knew I couldn't help him if I couldn't help myself first. I knew when I left him here that he was already into drugs. I started using at thirteen, and so did he. The difference between the two of us was when he started using, he also started dealing. He wasn't just dealing to the neighborhood kids. He was dealing with grown adults that my parents were dealing with. I'm now a mom of four, and I'm certain that if my fourteen-year-old has a wad of cash and no job, I'm going to question where that money came from, but it was never questioned. Nobody talked about it, because, you know, "We don't talk about those things." I moved away, and I started a better life for myself after I got married. After I had my first son, I told my husband, "I need to move back home. I need to be close to my dad." That gave us the opportunity to come back home. By that time, my brother was married. About a year after I got back, they had their first baby and then another year later he had a second baby. He and his wife were struggling. They had two kids. His addiction was full-blown. I got a phone call one night— it was about three o'clock in the morning—and I was pregnant with my second daughter. It was the Union City Police Department. The one thing that we all know about anybody who battles addiction, is that addicts are the greatest salespeople in the world. They can sell you anything at any given time, and he had convinced this police officer to call me, his sister, "she'll come and get me." That night I was very, very pregnant and there were flash flood warnings and tornado warnings. I had to call my husband. He worked the third shift and I said, "I need you to come home and sit with the baby. I've got to go get my brother." Of course, he was not happy about this because of all the weather threats, but he knew I was going to go. He knew this was my brother and that's just what it was. I got there and the police officer said, "He has two choices. He can go with you, and you can be responsible for him or he's going to jail." By the grace of God, he was not injured when he crashed his car that night. I told him, "You've got two choices. You're going to jail tonight, or tomorrow morning you're going to go to rehab, because you deserve something better. Your wife and your babies deserve something better." And he agreed to it. It was amazing because he went to rehab for thirty days clean and sober. This was the first time he had been clean and sober since he was thirteen, and I was so proud of him. Unfortunately, we all know when you come back home, everybody's still doing the exact same thing. Not everybody has the luxury of packing up and moving away. He knew he was going to struggle, and it was probably a month later he called me up and said, "Hey big sister, guess what I've done?" And I said, "Well, hell, I have no idea," because God only knew, right? And he said, "I joined the Army today." I will never forget that phone call. I was so proud of him. I was so proud of him knowing that he was fighting to break that cycle. He was fighting to give himself and his family a better life. It was just incredible. But again, we all know that the addiction gene doesn't leave us. He went into full-time military duty. And, well alcohol, it's part of their culture. It is what it is. He traded one addiction for another, but he was a functioning addict, right? He still went to work every single day, took care of his family, and was a great husband, great dad, and great uncle. Oh my gosh, my kids loved him. But part of being military is war, and war is ugly. During his first deployment, everything was fine. In his second deployment, we noticed things were a little off. We noticed his addiction was getting a little worse. I started getting those random phone calls at two or three in the morning where he was babbling and rambling. Nothing ever made sense. Then, on his third deployment, there was an IED explosion. He got a traumatic brain injury. He came home, and he was just never the same person. The VA had him so doped up. It was terrible. And watching someone you love turn into somebody that you don't recognize is gut-wrenching because there's nothing that you can do to save them. You can love them. You can encourage them. You can fight for them. But at the end of the day, they still have to fight for themselves. When the prescription pills got taken away because he was abusing them, he turned to street drugs. He started coke and heroin and meth and anything he could get his hands on. I just watched this incredible person's life get turned upside down. He lost every single material possession he owned. He lost his wife, and he lost custody of his kids. He became homeless. He would couch surf and stay in abandoned places or find somebody that knew someplace, and he would just stay here and there. It was terrible.

According to the Maryland Department of Health
- "70-80% of people with brain injuries leave inpatient rehabilitation with a prescription for opioids.
- An opioid is a drug that relieves pain. Prescription painkillers include oxycontin, Vicodin, morphine, and oxycodone. Fentanyl and heroin are also opioids.
- People who have had moderate to severe injuries are 10 times more likely to die from an overdose than those who don't.
- People with traumatic brain injuries are at much higher risk for opioid misuse and overdose."

(Maryland Department of Health. n.d. "Opioids and Brain Injury Facts" accessed May 21, 2023, https://health.maryland.gov/bha/Documents/Opioids%20and%20Brain%20Injury%20Facts.%20for%20individuals%20and%20families.pdf)

RANDY: How did you deal with that? How did you get involved? Because I know you did. I know you. Tell the folks what your thoughts were, your involvement, or your support, or your stepping away. You explain it.

JACKIE: I wish I could tell you that I was the best sister in the world, but I wasn't. Of course, I was involved. This was my little brother. It was just the two of us, and I loved him. I knew that deep down inside there was this incredibly amazing person so full of love, and he would have given anyone anything. If you came up to him and you needed a dollar and that's all he had, he would have given it to you. That's who he was. I tried to help him fight. It was hard. I wouldn't let him come and live at my house. I was trying to help his ex-wife take care of the kids because she was working all the time and the kids were little. I had my four kids and then her three kids by then, and I was working a full-time job. I was going crazy. I felt like I was losing my mind. I never turned my cell phone off. I was always afraid I was going to get that phone call. In the middle of this, my oldest son joined the military and ended up on

123

deployment to the exact same place where my brother was injured. That was terrifying. I would go days without sleeping because my brain just didn't want to turn off. I was always so afraid I was going to miss that phone call. There would be times that he would call his daughter and beg her for money. And she would call me, and she'd be crying and saying, "Aunt Jackie, please make him stop." I would just get so angry with him. I remember one day I had just had enough after getting a phone call from my niece where she was crying. I tracked him down. He was over in Hartford City or Upland at the time. I found him and we were screaming at each other face-to-face. I said one of the worst things you could ever say to somebody. I told him he was nothing but a worthless junkie. I said that because I was angry, and his children were hurting. My children were hurting. I knew he was hurting. But I just thought for one second, "Maybe. Maybe if I just make him mad enough, he'll see what the rest of us are seeing. Maybe he'll get that image of his children crying or my children crying or realizing what all of us are going through as we're watching him kill himself." Because literally, that's what it is. And you can't stop it. And he didn't see it that way. He had a few names for me. It was ugly. But the one thing that my brother and I always had, no matter how mad we were at each other—and I know it sounds ludicrous—we would always hug each other and say, "I love you" before we left. Always, even if we had been screaming at each other on the phone. It would be like, "OK, I'm done, but I love you," and we'd just hang up. I always wanted to make sure that if something happened, that was the last thing I said to him.

RANDY: That's powerful. We need to take that to heart. We can hate the moment. Better not hate the person. We can hate the situation, but we don't have to hate that person. And I think that's what I'm hearing you say right there. You could walk away knowing that even with all the anger and everything else you felt, the love was still there. That's why you kept returning to him and why he would return to you, even in the difficult moments. You said he was in the military, and after the explosion, he came home. I know you got a couple of calls during that time that you haven't mentioned yet. Tell us about some of those.

JACKIE: The first call that I got from him was in the middle of harvest. I work in Ag, and anybody who is a farmer or knows Ag at all knows that you work long hours, and you don't leave unless it's an emergency. I was over on the east side of Darke County. That's where I worked. I got a text message that said, "Hey big sister, I need you now. I've taken too much. I don't know if I'm going to make it." He didn't even have minutes on his phone for me to call him back. I remember thinking, "I have to get to him right now," and I couldn't call the police because there was no address. This was basically an abandoned building. I kept thinking, "OK, so if I call 911, what am I going to tell them? Like, OK, I know when I come into Hartford City, I turn right after the tracks and then there's a blue house and you turn left and then at the gas station you turn right, and then you go down…" They would have thought I was crazy. So, I just told my boss, "I've got to leave right now," and I got to him. Thank God he was still alive, and I took him straight to Marion to the VA. I was so disgusted. They wouldn't help us. The doctors and the nurses said, "We can't help him. He can't pass the drug screen." I said, "He's OD'ing. I know he can't pass the drug screen. We wouldn't be here if he could." They said, "Well bring him back in twenty-four to forty-eight hours, and if he can pass the drug screen then we can put him in rehab." I said, "That doesn't help me. In twenty-four to forty-eight hours, he'll be dead." I was terrified because nobody would help us, and I didn't know where to turn. There weren't places like Brianna's Hope. And at that time people still barely talked about addiction. I was so scared, and I remember just being so angry and crying. He said, "It'll be OK, big sister. I'll be fine. Just take me back." I remember thinking, "How selfish am I? I have a home that has heat and beds, and I'm letting my brother basically be homeless." But I just couldn't do it because I was so terrified that he would bring drugs into my house around our children. I couldn't do it. So, I took him back to where he was, and I dropped him off. I cried all the way home because there was nothing else I could do. And I live with that. I have to live with that every single day. Until you're in that position, you don't know what you would do. You don't know how that affects you and the things that you know could happen. A few months had gone by during this whole process, and in April 2013, our mother passed away. They were super close, the two of them. She and I were not. We did not have a good relationship—that's not a secret to anyone—but the two of them were super close. When she passed away unexpectedly, it changed his world. At the same time, our dad was going through stage four cancer. We knew we didn't have much time left with him, and I started to see the beginning of the end for my brother. He was never sober. He couldn't stay sober for a single day. A few months after that, our dad passed away. I remember being so angry at him because he showed up at my dad's memorial service so high, he didn't even know what day of the week it was. I was furious with him. I was livid, and I said, "One day. You can't give your family just one day of being clean." I was disgusted. I was angry. I still loved him. His heart was breaking just as bad as ours, but I was just so mad at him that day. I remember before he left, I begged him. I said, "I can't do this again. You're the only one I have left. I'm begging you to fight. There are so many places you can go. I'm begging you to get help. Your children deserve their dad. And he said, "I love you," and then left. Even as much as we would argue and fight, we did love each other unbelievably. We would still message each other every day. A few more months went by, and I got another phone call. He said, "Hey sister, I don't think I'm going to make it." So, I went and got him, and this time I took him to the Marion VA, and I refused to leave there until somebody helped us. It took us eight hours, two doctors, and six different nurses, but I refused to leave. I said, "Somebody has to help us. You know, he fought for his country. He deserves to be helped." They decided to help us, not because of his addiction, but because he had contracted Hep C from sharing dirty needles, and his liver was bad. It was shutting down. He was yellow. I remember his tongue was this weird, orange-yellow color, and he was sick. We found a hospital in Fort Wayne that was willing to take him, and I went with him. If you've never watched anyone detox, consider yourself grateful. It is tragic. One minute he was yelling and screaming and cussing at me, and the next minute he was telling me I'm his guardian angel and he's so thankful for me. I watched him puke on himself. I watched him urinate on himself. I watched him scream and holler. He finally went to sleep after about, I don't know, twelve or fourteen hours. He finally slept, and I told the nurse, "I'm going downstairs just long enough to get coffee. If he wakes up and he doesn't see me, he's going to freak. Please tell him I just went to get coffee." When I came back up, he was on his phone. And you know how in your gut, you just know something's going on. I said, "Gary Wade, let me have your phone." No, he wouldn't do it. And I knew he had texted his girlfriend. I knew in my gut that he had asked her to bring him some drugs. I told him, "If she's coming up here, I'm leaving. I'm not going to watch you kill yourself anymore. I can't do this. I can't bury another one. You know, we've buried both of our parents two years in a row. I can't lose you. I can't watch this." He begged me not to go. I went and I told the doctors and the nurses who this person was and what she was bringing in. Security was alerted, but they told us, "Sorry, we can't stop her. We have no reason to search her. He's the patient, and if he wants her in here, we can't stop that." I was livid. I felt like I was trying to fight for his life, and everything was going against us. When she came in, I told him, "You've got two choices. One of us is leaving." He was begging me not to leave him. I gave him a hug and a kiss, and I told him I loved him, and I said, "I'm begging you to fight. You have been through the worst. You can make it through this." The nurse was in there begging him not to leave, not to take anything, and just to keep fighting. He had already gone through the physical detox and now it was mental. But he wouldn't make his girlfriend leave, so I left. As I was walking out of his room he was screaming, "Jack, please don't leave me. I love you," but I walked out. It was the longest drive from Fort Wayne I had ever had in my life. I knew I was going to lose him. It was probably the longest time we've gone without talking to each other. It was probably about thirty days later that I got a call from him. He had checked himself into a VA rehab place in Fort Wayne. I was so proud of him, and I went to see him. I told him I loved him and that I was proud of him. I told him I was getting ready to have a major surgery, and I wasn't going to be able to drive for a few weeks, but if he needed anything, he could still call me, and Tim would take me to him. It was about four days after my surgery that I got a phone call from him, and I knew he was using again, because he said, "Why haven't you been to see me?" I said, "I told you I had surgery, and I couldn't come up." He said, "I didn't know you had surgery." I said, "When's the last time you used?" And he got so mad at me and said, "Why do you always ask me that?" I said, "Because I know you well enough." He became homeless again for a few months and was couch surfing with people. Finally, towards the end of May, or the beginning of June, the VA helped him find a house in Albany. I was so proud of him. June 1st was his birthday, so I went over to see him. We went grocery shopping, and we spent a couple of hours together. I told him I'd be back the following week to see him, but it ended up being almost two weeks before I could get over there. I went to see him, and I took him grocery shopping and we went out to eat. I remember we were sitting in McDonald's over there and he was twitching. He was jerking. He was having some withdrawals. He was super paranoid and he said, "We need to leave right now." I said, "Why?" He said, "Because they're talking about me." I didn't realize it, because I had just tuned everybody out, but he was right. There were people who could visibly see the addiction.

RANDY: They could see the struggle.

JACKIE: Yes. But what they didn't see—not a single person—was his veteran hat that he wore every single day. Nobody saw that. They saw the drug addict. They didn't see the dad. They didn't see the brother. They didn't see the uncle. They didn't see the soldier. They saw an addict.

RANDY: They didn't see a person. They saw a thing.

JACKIE: Yeah. It was terrible because I never realized how loud those whispers were before. I took him home and we sat there for a couple more hours and we talked about growing old and watching our babies grow up. I gave him a hug and a kiss. I told him I loved him, and I took this ridiculous selfie of the two of us. He was so annoyed. He said, "You and your selfies. You're driving me crazy." But I knew I needed it. That coming weekend was Father's Day weekend. He was supposed to pick up his youngest son. He didn't. He wasn't returning anybody's phone calls. Sunday was Father's Day, but he still didn't return anybody's phone calls. I knew in my gut something was wrong. On Monday morning I got a phone call from his ex-mother-in-law, and she said, "Jack, Bub's gone." I said, "OK, where did he go now?" And she's like, "No, Jack. Rumor has it Bub is gone." I said, "What do you mean?" She said that he had OD'd. I left work. I called the Albany Police Department. I had to leave a voice message. I called the Delaware County Sheriff to see what I could find out. I called the Delaware County Coroner. I got about halfway to Albany when the Albany police officer called me and confirmed they had found him that morning. He had OD'd in his apartment. I had to call his ex-wife's work so she could go get the boys. His daughter was living with me. I had to go pull her out of a factory and tell her she was never going to see her dad again. This young girl looks right at me, and she just knew. I didn't have to say a word. And this poor little girl, she just puked everywhere. It was just too much. Sitting with my niece and nephews for the next couple of days planning a funeral was terrible. It was just awful. They were too young. They shouldn't have had to experience that.

"Gary McCowan, age 40, a former Redkey resident, passed away on Monday, June 22, 2015, at his home in Albany."

"Gary was born on June 1, 1975, in Portland, the son of Arthur Gary and Betty Louann (Cline) McCowan. He graduated in 1993 from Jay County High School. Gary was a veteran of the U.S. Army serving in Iraq and Afghanistan. He was a member of the Redkey American Legion. "

"Survivors include daughter, Tasha McCowan of Redkey, Indiana, two sons, Elijah McCowan of Redkey, Indiana and Jacob McCowan of Redkey, Indiana, and sister, Jackie Sheridan (husband Tim) of Ft. Recovery, Ohio"

(Williamson-Spencer Funeral Home. n.d. "Gary Wade McCowan" accessed May 21, 2023,

RANDY: Jackie, tell the folks what his last moments were like that you're aware of. Obviously, you weren't there. But you do know some of what took place and how his final moments played out.

JACKIE: I ended up working with the Albany police officer. They had discovered his body because somebody had broken in that morning to get the rest of the drugs out of the house before his body was found. Somebody drove by and saw someone sneak in the window, and that's how he was discovered.

RANDY: So, hold on. Somebody was with him the night before. At least one somebody, and I believe there's reason to believe there were multiple people. And the way his body was found. They didn't call it in that he had passed out or that he had died. They were breaking in to get the drugs they had left there the night before?

JACKIE: That is true. He always said he had what he called "ride-or-die buddies". And I know a lot of people use that comment. I despise it because his buddies rode off into the sunset and left him to die alone. What I do know is this—and this is what gives me peace, and a lot of people didn't realize this—my brother had been saved and baptized. He believed in God, and he told me every single time we would talk for the last year of his life that he prayed that God would take this away from him. Well, God did take this away from him, just not the way that we wanted Him to. But I know he's no longer suffering and he's no longer battling those demons. It just so happens that when I was at the police department, I looked on the computer screen and there was a folder of pictures, an icon on the desktop, that had my brother's name. I told the police officer I wanted to see them. And he said, "I'm sorry ma'am, we don't show those." I said, "You don't understand. Drugs have been a part of my life since the day I was born. I have lost too many family members to drugs. I need this for closure. I need to see those photos." He said, "You need to understand, we have to take photos when we come in and we find a body." I said, "I know, but something's telling me, I have to see this." My brother was found on his knees, with his elbows on the bed and his head in his hands and it looked like he was praying. At that very moment in time, I knew exactly what he had prayed for, and I knew that God had answered his prayers. That's what gives me peace, because I know he's safe and I know he's free, and he deserved that.

RANDY: Folks, I don't know what your faith tells you. I don't know how you read some of the scriptures. I don't know what your takeaway is. But I know what my takeaway is from this moment and this story. God doesn't always work in the way we want him to. God always works. We may not see it, but it doesn't mean he's not working. He may not bring our healing when wearing this body, but there's a far better healing awaiting us. Nobody wants to lose a loved one, especially through this kind of struggle and turmoil and hurt and loss. But I also knew Gary and he was a friend. I saw that conflict within him. And we tried as so many did. But as you know, it belongs to them. We can only offer. It's like, "Here's a gift, you've got to reach out and take it." Gary was a gift to us. Those last moments, let those define who he was, instead of that mumbling in McDonald's. I'm not picking on McDonald's. That just happened to be the location that day. But recognize and realize that God sees us on the inside and out. We see people just on the outside. We don't know what's going on in their minds and hearts, or what they are struggling with. Jackie, it was powerful how you shared this and talked about that being your moment of peace and hope for the future. Where are you today? How's life playing out for you?

JACKIE: Life is amazing. Brianna's Hope started, and you gave me this great opportunity about thirty days after Gary Wade passed away to share our story. I could have never imagined in my wildest dreams where that would have taken us. Here we are, what, six or seven years later? I've shared our story with thousands of people all over Indiana and Ohio. It's been amazing to hear other people say, "Thank you," to hear people say, "Thank you for offering us hope." I've lived this life. I've grown up the same way you did, so I know that you can make it out of there. I graduated college. I've raised four children. This year, I'm going to celebrate thirty years of marriage to this incredibly strong man who can deal with me, and I'm blessed. My niece and nephews are doing incredible. Their dad would be so proud of them, and I don't think it gets any better than that. We miss him. Two of my oldest children were in the military. They followed in their uncle's footsteps. His children are doing so great and working. His daughter graduated, and she's married. His oldest son just bought a house and I'm just so proud of them. His baby is going to graduate here in a few months. They're all moving on with their lives, and that's all that you can ask for. We'll never forget him. We will always love him, and we're grateful for the years that we had.

RANDY: Absolutely. I was privileged and honored to do Gary's memorial service. It was held at the VA Cemetery in Marion, Indiana. It was my first one there. And just to stand there and look out across those white tombstones and salute the past, the present, and the future was incredible. Gary McCowan, I salute you today. And Jackie, thank you. Thank you for sharing your heart and being raw and being real. Thank you for continuing to give folks hope.

JACKIE: Thank you. I take every opportunity as a blessing and I'm forever grateful for that.

RANDY: Shouldn't we all? We, all of us, need to. Listen to these final words we like to close with so often, and I hope you'll do it: Stay in the battle.

ACE Quiz

"For each "yes" answer, add one. The total number at the end is your cumulative number of ACEs. Before your eighteenth birthday:

1. Did a parent or other adult in the household often or very often... Swear at you, insult you, put you down, or humiliate you? Or act in a way that made you afraid that you might be physically hurt?

2. Did a parent or other adult in the household often or very often... Push, grab, slap, or throw something at you? Or ever hit you so hard that you had marks or were injured?

3. Did an adult or person at least 5 years older than you ever... Touch or fondle you or have you touch their body in a sexual way? Or attempt or actually have oral, anal, or vaginal intercourse with you?

4. Did you often or very often feel that ... No one in your family loved you or thought you were important or special? Or your family didn't look out for each other, feel close to each other, or support each other?

5. Did you often or very often feel that ... You didn't have enough to eat, had to wear dirty clothes, and had no one to protect you? Or your parents were too drunk or high to take care of you or take you to the doctor if you needed it?

6. Were your parents ever separated or divorced?

7. Was your mother or stepmother often or very often pushed, grabbed, slapped, or had something thrown at her? Or sometimes, often, or very often kicked, bitten, hit with a fist, or hit with something hard? Or ever repeatedly hit over at least a few minutes or threatened with a gun or knife?

8. Did you live with anyone who was a problem drinker or alcoholic, or who used street drugs?

Continued...

9. Was a household member depressed or mentally ill, or did a household member attempt suicide?
10. Did a household member go to prison?"

"An ACE score is a tally of different types of abuse, neglect, and other adverse childhood experiences. A higher score indicates a higher risk for health problems later in life."

(Center on the Developing Child: Harvard University. "Take the ACE Quiz – And Learn What It Does and Doesn't Mean" accessed May 21, 2023, https://developingchild.harvard.edu/media-coverage/take-the-ace-quiz-and-learn-what-it-does-and-doesnt-mean)

Chapter 8

Kourtney Thompson — "Now I realize I don't have to be drunk to have a good time."

"Wine is a mocker, strong drink a brawler, and whoever is led astray by it is not wise."
(Proverbs 20:1 NIV)

At just nine years old, Kourtney Thompson had her first taste of alcohol. By the time she was fourteen, she was drinking from the moment she woke up until she couldn't even stand up at night. After witnessing her mother's abusive relationship, she found herself in an abusive relationship of her own when she tried to make her escape from a neglectful home at just eighteen. She says that she was drinking to "speed up the process" because she didn't want to be alive anymore. Everything turned around when she found her bonus family. She now celebrates nine months sober and is prepared to continue her sobriety journey with the help of the people she surrounds herself with today.

RANDY: I'm your host, Randy Davis, a pastor as well as founder and executive director of A Better Life - Brianna's Hope. We're a participant-driven, faith-based, compassion-filled, support recovery movement for those battling the battle with substance use disorder/addiction. Our guest today comes all the way from the beautiful town of Berne, Indiana, over there in Adams County. Welcome, Kourtney Thompson.

KOURTNEY: Nice to be here.

RANDY: Well, we're excited to have you and looking forward to hearing your story. We want to get your experiences in life, what the battle was like for you and how the victory is looking right now. I realize the battle is not over. We recognize that, but it sounds to me like you're in a good place currently. Do you agree?

KOURTNEY: Yeah, I think so!

RANDY: Awesome. OK, well go ahead and introduce yourself to our listeners. Tell us a little something about you in the present day.

KOURTNEY: I'm twenty years old, and I'm a recovering alcoholic. Through Brianna's Hope, I have found a bonus family and a support team. I wouldn't be where I am today without them.

RANDY: Great. Tell the folks what you mean by a bonus family.

KOURTNEY: Well, for a lot of people I know, and for me personally, we don't have a family anymore that accepts us. We call our Brianna's Hope family our bonus family because they support us, love us, and do anything they can to help us and be there for us, no matter what. They've become a big part of my life, and they're pretty much the only family I have. I appreciate all of them.

RANDY: It sounds to me like they fill a big void, yes?

KOURTNEY: Yes.

RANDY: That's powerful. That means a lot. Who among us isn't searching for some kind of connection and acceptance? So many times, not having that is what drives folks to that dark side, because we will all find acceptance in one place or the other. Let's go back in your life. Tell us how you got started with alcohol.

KOURTNEY: I started drinking when I was nine years old, and drinking regularly by the time I was fourteen or fifteen. I would drink until I couldn't stand up anymore. I was drinking from the time I woke up until the time I went to bed. Alcohol was always something that I had around. I started smoking cigarettes and weed when I was thirteen, and that continued until recently. I just hit my nine months sober from alcohol and everything.

RANDY: Congratulations! That's big.

KOURTNEY: Yeah.

RANDY: You say you started at the age of nine. It was always around? It was available in your household, is that correct?

KOURTNEY: Yes, and my friends always had stuff. People at school always had stuff. My family always had stuff in the house. It was just easily accessible.

136

"Many youth have easy access to alcohol. In 2019, among adolescents ages 12 to 14 who reported drinking alcohol in the past month, 96.5 percent reported getting it for free the last time they drank. In many cases, adolescents have access to alcohol through family members or find it at home."

(National Institute on Alcohol Abuse and Alcoholism. n.d. "Alcohol's Effects on Health" accessed May 22, 2023, https://www.niaaa.nih.gov/publications/brochures-and-fact-sheets/underage-drinking)

RANDY: You made it clear that you would drink from daylight to dark. How was life going for you at that point? What was school like, and the other relationships outside your household?

KOURTNEY: When I was fourteen, I had just finished eighth grade. My mom got married the summer after eighth grade, and we moved to Fort Wayne. That meant starting a new school for high school. I went into it not knowing anybody, and by about halfway through my sophomore year, I was drinking all the time. I found people to party with, smoke with, whatever. Whether it was just stepping outside the school building or people I rode the bus with or whatever, I found people to fit in with. I didn't do it just to fit in. I was trying to drown out all the other stuff I had going on at home. That strained my relationship with a few of my good friends because they didn't like seeing me like that.

RANDY: You must have gone through a series of adverse childhood experiences, yes?

KOURTNEY: Yes

RANDY: You used substances to cover up that pain and cover it over. At the time they must have felt like good moments, even when you look back and see that they weren't so good. Is that accurate?

KOURTNEY: There were times when I knew it wasn't helping and I knew I wasn't facing everything. I didn't really care because I didn't even want to necessarily be alive. I did anything to kind of speed up the process.

RANDY: OK, that's understandable. Obviously, you went through a lot of pain, and this was a way to numb that. You were in a rough time, no doubt. You said you began with alcohol, then you moved to cigarettes and marijuana. Was that with the group that had accepted you, that group of friends? Or did that come about in a different way?

KOURTNEY: Actually, I started smoking weed with my friend's dad when we were thirteen years old. He had me trick her into thinking I had already smoked with him before because I would stay with them all the time. My mom would leave for weeks or a month at a time and I'd just be in my apartment by myself. I would go upstairs to my friend's apartment. I would stay there most of the time, so I wouldn't be alone. He had his daughter come over the next day and he's like, "Oh, just, like, go along with it, go along with it." Then he packs a pipe or whatever, a bowl of weed, and rolls a joint. He looked at his daughter and said, "Oh, well she already smoked with me last night. So, do you want to hit this?" She smoked first. I thought since I had already supposedly done it, I had to do it. That's how I got started smoking weed. Before that, we had already been stealing cigarettes from her mom and stuff like that. Her mom worked at a gas station, so she always brought home boxes of cigarettes and everything.

RANDY: Because of the access it made it easy for you and your friend to get what you wanted.

KOURTNEY: Yes.

RANDY: Where did it go from there? You started with your friend and her dad. Where did your battle with weed and marijuana take you?

KOURTNEY: Honestly, it got me in a lot more trouble than I'd like to admit. Never legally because I guess I was just careful about not getting caught. I would find people that I knew smoked, whether they were older than me or not. I would find friends of friends and I'd smoke with them, or I would ask kids at school, "Hey, I know you smoke, where do you get your weed?" I'd buy some from them or they'd hook me up with a dealer, and I'd hook up with a dealer. I was selling for a little bit, not in large quantities, but I was lucky to never get caught. I would never do it again. I would do that just to make money to buy food. I'd sell dime bags out of my house. I would just run them outside of my mom's house and slip them over and they'd slip me the money. Then, I would just run back inside my house and continue smoking on the supply I was selling.

RANDY: I'm going to say for lack of better words, that's the way you were making it through life at the moment.

KOURTNEY: Yes. 100 percent.

RANDY: OK. Take us forward from there. Was what you just described during junior high or high school?

KOURTNEY: It was the end of junior high and the beginning of high school, for the most part. I smoked weed all through high school and afterwards. I really, really started drinking when my stepdad came around. He was a very violent drunk. He always had alcohol in the house. He was always on something. He was always starting fights with my mom or with me and he'd put his hands on her and stuff. He slipped me liquor bottles. One time, he flipped their truck three times. I remember waking up that morning because we had a two-hour delay or a cancellation or something at school. The text message alert about that woke me up, and I remember hearing them pull out of the parking lot to go to work. I remember thinking, "Oh they're going to wreck." Then about an hour later I got a phone call, and my stepdad was crying. He was like, "We flipped the truck. Your mom's hurt," and all this and that. He picked me up like five hours later. He was already shit-faced drunk, like absolutely wasted. He took me to the hospital with his mom to go see my mom. She had shattered her femur because they didn't have their seat belts on. That was a kind of a control thing on his part, so I wasn't necessarily surprised. He pulled a bunch of shot bottles out of his coat pockets, and he said, "Here, go in the bathroom and drink these," because he knew I didn't like hospitals. He said, "It'll mellow you out." And I said, "OK." I went in the bathroom of the hospital, and I downed four shots. It was nothing. It was always liquor. It was never beer for me. It was always hard liquor, whether it was whiskey, vodka,

139

tequila, or whatever. It was always the harder stuff because it worked faster. It worked better.

RANDY: Your access was overwhelming, it sounds like. As you look back at that time in your life, did you have anyone you would say was supporting you in a positive way? Any kind of, as you referred to earlier, bonus family? A grandparent or neighbor, an uncle, brother, or sister? Did you have anybody on your side that was working to get you into a positive place in your life?

KOURTNEY: Michael Bear and a select few high school teachers. I had a neighbor who would always give me food and everything, because I was sixteen, and my stepdad almost beat the life out of my mom.

RANDY: Did you see that happen?

KOURTNEY: Yes. I'm the one that called the police, and after that, there was a protective order put in place. When they caught him, my mom was mad at me for calling the police. I said, "Well, I'm going to leave." I was going to leave with my boyfriend at the time. I said, "I'm not going to be here to watch you die. I'm not. If you don't want to leave, that is on you. That is your choice. You're an adult, but that is not love. Nobody that loves you is going to do that to you." I said, "So I'm either going to leave after I help you go somewhere safe, or you're going to stay here and when I get back, you're going to be dead. But that is not my fault. I am not the person that's supposed to save you."

RANDY: Let me interrupt you just a minute. I want to go back to that moment when you called the police. You're sixteen at this time. Where did that kind of wisdom come from to be able to deal with it on those terms?

KOURTNEY: I've been seeing it and dealing with it for most of my life, not just from him, but from previous men that she had been married to or in relationships with. Whether the violence was directed at me or at her, it just became normal. Honestly, it was just a regular thing, like, "Same stuff, different day."

RANDY: OK, now let's go back. You said you called the police.

KOURTNEY: My mom was screaming at me. I went over to my neighbor's house, and I didn't cry at all until I got in her door.

I pounded on her door, and I walked in, and she said, "What's going on?" She heard yelling and stuff breaking and she didn't know what was going on. She's older. She was in her sixties, and she said, "Honey, are you okay?" I said, "I just called the cops. Can I sit here for a little bit until they get here?" She said, "Yeah, of course." Then she hugged me, and I just started bawling because I guess that's when I was able to actually let it out.

RANDY: You had to be in protection and defensive mode up to that moment, and you felt like she gave you permission to let go.

KOURTNEY: Yeah.

RANDY: Let's go forward from there. What were the results of that?

KOURTNEY: My mom moved out for seven months. There was a protective order put in place, which she did not follow. She moved out of our house and left me there to finish my junior year by myself and start my senior year by myself. I paid for my whole senior year of high school on my own. I got a job at a Subway that was connected to a gas station by my house. I would walk there along the highway every day. It was a fifteen to twenty-minute walk, and I would show up drunk. I would put liquor in my coffee and take it to work with me. I would smoke before I got to work, and I'd take a couple of anxiety pills not prescribed to me. I would just show up at work, and I would pay my mom's bills, and I'd pay for my school. I would try to pay for my food if I could, but that was a long walk to get to a store.

RANDY: Wow. That's a bunch right there. Did you say that was your junior and senior years? The school had to notice. Obviously, you've already mentioned some teachers you were able to get close with. Did they come to you, or did you go to them?

KOURTNEY: A little bit of both. Some of them noticed that something was wrong and there was a kid that told on me, which I was very upset with at the time. I would self-harm, and I guess they saw the cuts on my arm. The guidance counselor pulled me out of class, and she asked, "What is going on?" I told her a little bit and DCS got involved. I think I had seven cases in my junior year, but they never did anything because I was going to age out of the system, and they couldn't really do anything anyways. They gave my mom a heads up before they did a house visit. So, of course, she came early before they showed up. She would come back to the house, and she'd fill the fridge with food because it had been empty for the most part. She just acted like everything was fine, like she'd been there this whole time. So, they didn't do anything. I was just stuck there until I graduated.

"Cutting is actually a form of addiction as many teenagers crave the release that self-harm behaviors elicit. Studies have shown that it can be an outlet for an escape allowing teens to release negative feelings of anger, frustration, sadness and stress. However, once this act is over, teenagers crave more, just like an addictive drug."

"Studies have shown that approximately nine percent of teenagers who engage in self-harming behaviors also abuse drugs and alcohol. Teenagers abuse drugs and alcohol for similar reasons they engage in self-harm behavior; to alleviate stress and numb the pain and emotions they are experiencing. Marijuana and nonmedical prescription drugs are the most commonly abused illicit substances among teenagers with alcohol and tobacco being the most commonly abused substances overall."

"Drugs and alcohol are known to slow reaction times, increase impulsivity and disrupt the connections in nerve endings potentially resulting in worsening injuries. For example, individuals who cut may cut too deep under the influence of drugs or alcohol resulting in serious wounds or too much blood loss."

(Discovery Mood & Anxiety Program. n.d. "Teenage Addiction and Self-Harm: Co-occuring Disorders" accessed May 22, 2023, https://discoverymood.com/blog/teenage-addiction-self-harm-co-occurring-disorders)

"Student drug abuse often falls under responsibilities related to student safety and associated prevention measures. When a child is in school, the teachers, administrators, and other staff members on campus are responsible for the student's safety and well-being while the student is on campus. From a legal standpoint, federal and state laws have been put in place to create drug-free schools where any type of illicit or addictive substances are banned. Prescription medications that are necessary for the treatment of a medical condition are usually excluded, but only if they meet certain requirements laid out in policies placed by the school, district, or local or state government. It is often the responsibility of any staff or student on a school campus to report violations to school administrators, who often address such situations and contact authorities when necessary."

"Teachers may also have some responsibility to address student drug abuse under mandatory reporting laws. These laws are applicable to cases of child neglect and abuse where certain individuals, like educators, are expected to report instances to the proper authorities. However, the circumstances of a student's drug use may constitute an application of mandated reporting."

"If the parent(s) are exposing or otherwise supplying their child with drugs, it may be deemed as abuse under the law as they are jeopardizing their child's safety, which makes it a mandatory reporting situation for the teacher. A report would also be necessary when the parent(s) abuse drugs, as there can be suspected abuse and neglect. Indirect or unintentional drug exposure can be included, as a home-based production of methamphetamine can expose everyone in the home to the drug's toxins."

(On the Wagon. n.d. "Identifying Drug Abuse Among Students: A Guide for Teachers" accessed May 22, 2023, https://www.onthewagon.org/guide-for-teachers/)

RANDY: It's incredible that you were able to graduate from high school with all that stuff going on.

KOURTNEY: Yeah. School was my way out. That was the only way I had out whether I went to college or not. I knew I needed to graduate, and I almost didn't. I really, really pushed myself, and I had people that pushed me to do it.

RANDY: Wow. That's amazing that you could have done that. Congratulations for that effort and the recognition of how bad you needed that diploma. That's big. Take us forward from your high school days. That was only a couple of years ago, so there's not a lot of space there. But take us forward, please.

KOURTNEY: I got into a really bad relationship. I graduated high school early, and I moved out ten days after I graduated. I didn't even know that I would have a place to stay. I was couch hopping for a little while, and then I reconnected with a guy that I had been on and off with since I was fourteen.

RANDY: Did he know your story?

KOURTNEY: Yes, he did. He ended up being very abusive and not very supportive of me in my recovery journey. My bonus family saved me a little bit because he put his hands on me. I went to the church because I didn't know where else to go. I just walked out one day, and I had bruises from my shoulders down to my knees.

RANDY: From the physical altercation?

KOURTNEY: Yes, and there were multiple altercations. But he was supposed to love me. I almost got married to him. He helped me stop drinking for the first time and I thought that everything was going to be good, and I was going to be happy and everything. But his issues were kind of overriding everything.

RANDY: So, you kind of got into the situation that your mom had been living before you.

KOURTNEY: Yes, and he was not the first one like that.

RANDY: OK.

KOURTNEY: And he wasn't the last.

RANDY: Well, you made a comment a minute ago. He wasn't in support of your recovery journey. How did that journey start?

KOURTNEY: I had left him and got back with him. The first time I left him, Michael Bear invited me to a meeting. I went, but going to a meeting the first time, I thought, "I don't need this. There's nothing wrong with me." After a lot of self-reflection and thinking about it, I realized that I am an alcoholic and that I do need help. I don't want to be the person I was when I was drinking heavily every day.

RANDY: How many meetings did you go to before you got that personal revelation of, "I do have some things I need to deal with."

KOURTNEY: Honestly, it probably took me a couple of months to fully accept that. I kept going, but there were times where I'd skip meetings. I relapsed once, but I got right back up, and I showed up to a meeting. I said, "Hey guys, I messed up."

RANDY: How'd they deal with that?

KOURTNEY: They took me back in with open arms. They were like, "That's OK. As long as you get back up, and you're sitting here, you're owning up to your mistake and you're trying again. That's what matters."

RANDY: Yeah, I think of the scriptures, and I think of the story of Peter and how many times he stumbled, fell, and relapsed in behaviors. But he got up one more time than he was down. You know what folks, if you were here with me and you could see Kourtney, you'd see there's nothing physical, as far as large size goes. She's a tiny gal. And I say all of that to say this strength is on the inside, not in your biceps or other parts of your body. And she's flexing them now, I think. I don't know. But regardless, she found strength. She found support. She found help. Take us forward in your recovery journey please, once you realized you had some folks you could count on.

KOURTNEY: After I relapsed, I started going back to meetings again, and I ended up getting back in a relationship with that guy. He set me back a little bit, not in my recovery journey, but in my healing of myself, with my trauma and everything else. He was just causing more damage and I left him again for the last time. Now I am nine months sober—almost ten—and I'm happier. I'm healthier. I feel better about myself, and I know that there are

145

people who are so proud of me. On countless occasions, I've had people say, "You are so different from when you first started coming to meetings," because I wouldn't talk. I'd just sit there with my head down. I wouldn't really interact with anybody. I don't really like being touched and now I'll go up and be like, "Oh, do you need a hug?" If I'm having a good day, I'm OK with it, you know? I have my boundaries and everything, but they've been such a good thing for me, honestly. I probably wouldn't be here without them. I probably would have drunk myself to death, and I'm glad I didn't.

RANDY: Yes. So are we and so is everybody listening. What kind of advice would you give to someone who's in an abusive relationship where drugs and or alcohol is involved? What would you say to them?

KOURTNEY: Those people don't love you if they can hurt you like that. Or if they're pushing drugs and alcohol on you and saying, "Oh, do this. It'll be fun. You're more of a fun person if you do this." Don't ever conform to what somebody else's expectations are of you.

RANDY: I love that line. Don't ever conform to what someone else's expectations of you are.

KOURTNEY: Yes. Because if they want to change who you are or make you a worse person. If they want to push you deeper into your addictions or your alcoholism or whatever. If they want to just push you around in general, they do not love you. They do not care about you. They do not support you. You need to be supported and cared about.

RANDY: They just want to dominate and take control of you. I heard it said years and years ago that those who want to control have lost control themselves. Controlling others is a way for them to feel better. They think, "If I can one up you and stand above you, I can take charge of your life even if I can't take charge of my own."

KOURTNEY: I never want to see somebody go through feeling or dealing with what I went through. Even as a teenager in abusive relationships, I was pushed to the point where I didn't think I should be here anymore. I thought that nobody was ever going to love me because that sure as heck wasn't love. I tried to take the easy way out and I tried to kill myself at least three times. But I'm still here.

RANDY: What kept that from happening?

KOURTNEY: I woke up. That's it. I logically should not be alive. The last time I attempted, I cut up both my arms, my legs, my hips, and my stomach. I took 200 anxiety pills, and I downed them with alcohol. I woke up the next day bloody and stuck to my sheets or my floor wherever I passed out. I think maybe I threw up once from it and that was it. I was mad. I was very, very angry that I woke up, because I did not want to wake up. But I did. I am not religious, but I do believe that everything happens for a reason, and I woke up for a reason.

RANDY: Maybe today's that reason. There is a scripture passage that says that we were basically created for such a moment as this and which you have had to say. There's got to be people out there who can relate, who have been in that extreme darkness and have either intentionally or unintentionally tried to take their own life. I can understand that a little, not that I've been there. But my mother was successful in taking her own life, so I can relate to some of what you're saying. I'm just thrilled you were a failure at it, which makes you a success, because look what you have to give now. What are your hopes? What are your plans for the future? What's your dream? I don't care how big it is.

KOURTNEY: I just want to help people. That's why I'm here telling my story. That's why I've told my story at our Brianna's Hope chapter. It helps me to get it out there and everything. If I can help somebody else—whether they can relate to my story, or they have questions, or they're thinking about doing something in terms of pills, alcohol, weed, or hurting themselves—I can be there and try to help them through that feeling or that craving or whatever. To cope with my own self-harm, I tattoo myself because it's a way of turning my pain into something beautiful.

RANDY: What's your favorite tattoo that you have?

KOURTNEY: I didn't do this one, but there's a tree on my arm that is for my sister that was stillborn. That is my favorite tattoo. When she was cremated, we got a tree and at her headstone, we planted the tree and put her ashes around it. It was like she was still growing and still living with us in a way. I have a tattoo of her tree with her name under it to remind me that she's with me all the time.

RANDY: Would you mind sharing her name?

KOURTNEY: Tara. It means earth, so I thought that was fitting.

RANDY: Ashes to ashes. Dust to dust. Earth to earth and there's the tree to prove it. OK, wow. Thank you for sharing that. That's personal. We appreciate that. You have been through quite a bit of darkness and hurt and struggles and battles to be only twenty years old. But let me say this: I hope you can figure out what it's about. I've dealt with folks in here who just started to turn their lives around in their thirties or forties or even later. I am not diminishing what you've been through, but I'm applauding you for getting it stopped and moving forward as you are at this point. Tell the folks out there who are on the verge of making that decision between remaining with their struggle and continuing to drink or to use versus going to some sort of recovery element.

KOURTNEY: Continuing to drink or use or whatever is just prolonging the inevitable. Honestly, it is trying to drown out something that only sends you back farther and it comes back crashing in waves. It's like a hurricane hitting you all at once, once you're sober again and that's why you keep drinking. That's why you keep using. It's to try to numb it out, but it always comes back at least twenty times harder.

RANDY: What has been the joy of your recovery up to this point?

KOURTNEY: Getting to realize that I don't have to be drunk or high or tripping or whatever to have a good time, or to be accepted by people, or to feel like I'm wanted where I am.

RANDY: That's good stuff, Kourtney. Let me close with this question. I know you said you're not a religious person, and that's not an issue here at *Faith In Your Recovery*. But what does that title, *Faith In Your Recovery,* mean to you?

KOURTNEY: You have to believe in something, and you have to believe in yourself. You have to believe in the people helping you through your recovery so you can actually recover, because if you don't believe that you can do it, you're not going to do it.

RANDY: Well said. You're wise beyond your years. You've done a tremendous job sharing your experiences with us. You know, you said you wanted to grow up to make a difference. You're an adult. I get that. But you're still a young adult. You made a difference here today. Thank you for your boldness and willingness. We talked earlier about how, like a lot of people, you have "microphobia"—fear of the microphone—but you have handled yourself extremely well and we're pleased with that. Thank you.

KOURTNEY: Thank you.

RANDY: Folks, just when you're at your worst, God shows up with his best. Your setbacks are a setup for your comeback. Kourtney has shared her powerful story with us today on *Faith In Your Recovery*, and we hope it's impacted you and that you will move forward in your journey toward recovery. God bless you. Stay in the battle.

Contact Page

- The *Faith In Your Recovery* podcast - a new episode airs each Friday at 6:00am eastern time and can be found on all leading podcast platforms.
- Would you or someone you know make a good interview for our podcast?
- Interested in knowing more about our Recovery Movement?
- Interested in opening a chapter of ABLBH in your community?
- Interested in having a speaker at your organization?
- Interested in becoming a volunteer?

Contact us in any of the following ways!

Organization website: ablbh.org

Book website: recoveryconversations.org

Office address: 115 E. Water St.

Portland, IN 47371

Office email: info@ablbh.org

Podcast email: podcast@ablbh.org

Office phone: (260) 766-2006

All proceeds from the sale of this book will be used to meet the recovery needs of those dealing with Substance Use Disorder/Addiction.

A B L B H
A Better Life: Brianna's Hope

Made in the USA
Monee, IL
13 July 2023